RAINFORESTS

An Activity Guide for Ages 6–9

Nancy F. Castaldo

CHICAGO
REVIEW
PRESS

Library of Congress Cataloging-in-Publication Data

Castaldo, Nancy F. (Nancy Fusco), 1962–

    Rainforests : an activity guide for ages 6–9 / Nancy F. Castaldo.—1st ed.

        p. cm.

    Summary: Provides facts and activities that explore tropical and temperate ancient forests, discusses how individuals can help preserve them, and describes well-known and unfamiliar creatures of the rainforest.

    Includes bibliographical references (p. 114).

    ISBN 1-55652-476-5

    1. Rain forests—Study and teaching—Activity programs—Juvenile literature.   2. Rain forest ecology—Study and teaching—Activity programs—Juvenile literature. [1. Rain forests. 2. Rain forest ecology. 3. Ecology.] I. Title.

QH86 .C365 2003

577.34—dc21

                                                      2002152661

Cover and interior design: Monica Baziuk

Cover and interior illustration: B. Kulak

First edition

Published by Chicago Review Press, Incorporated

814 North Franklin Street

Chicago, Illinois 60610

ISBN 1-55652-476-5

Printed in the United States of America

5   4   3   2   1

For those who dream of faraway forests and those who fight for their survival.

CONTENTS

ACKNOWLEDGMENTS

Many thanks to my dad for giving me the names of the trees, and to my mom for opening my mind to these marvelous forests. Thanks to Dolores Mannix for sharing her love and knowledge of the rainforests of South America, architect Geoff Miles for teaching me about the architecture of buttresses, and Kevin Russell, founder of the Rainforest Awareness Project, for his insights on the Borneo rainforests. Special thanks to Lisa Rosenthal and Cynthia Sherry for their enthusiasm and support. And always to Dean and Lucie for their constant love and encouragement.

INTRODUCTION

"In all things of nature there is something of the marvelous."
—Aristotle

The Greek philosopher Aristotle wrote these words over 2,000 years ago. And although Aristotle may never have traveled to a rainforest, his words certainly resound in the minds of all who have experienced these truly marvelous places. Rainforests are the oldest kind of forest. They have been growing on our planet for millions of years. They are home to the largest concentration of animals, birds, and insects on earth. In fact, some rainforest creatures haven't even been named yet! Rainforests give our world enormous amounts of oxygen and store two-thirds of its fresh water. They give us medicines, spices, fruits, nuts, and chocolate. What could be more marvelous?

Most rainforests are near the equator. Those are called *tropical* rainforests. Others are farther away from the equator and are called *temperate* rainforests. These are found in places such as the Pacific Northwest of the United States and in parts of New Zealand. Both types of rainforests have a tremendous amount of rainfall each year and the same layers, including the forest floor, understory, canopy, and emergent. But they differ greatly in the variety of plants and animals they support.

Rainforests is written for everyone who marvels at these rainforests, whether or not you have visited one. Alone or in groups, you will enjoy the activities that explore these tropical and temperate ancient forests. You will also discover how you can help preserve them. You'll learn about creatures you may never have heard of and also about some familiar favorites. Facts will pop out in Rainforest Reflection sidebars, and ideas for more fun appear in Rainforest Challenges at the end of the book. Most of all, you will discover a new frontier that they'll want to explore again and again. So turn the page and start getting wild about rainforests!

THE FOREST FLOOR
1

Have you ever taken a hike in the woods? Think about what you see and hear there. The ground under your feet might be rocky or covered with leaves. Sunlight might be streaming down through the leaves of the trees to the ground at your feet. You may find deciduous trees, which lose their leaves in the fall, and evergreen trees, which stay green all through the winter. You could wrap your arms around most of the tree trunks you see. It might be quiet on your hike or you might hear a bird or two. Now imagine you have traveled to a rainforest. The word rainforest was created in 1903 to describe forests that grow in constantly wet conditions. In rainforests the rainfall is more than 80 inches (2 m) a year.

You would find many differences between a rainforest and other forests that grow in drier or more temperate conditions. Rainforests are made up of many more layers than the temperate forests that might be near your home. The first layer of the rainforest is called the *forest floor*, and it's the first layer that we'll explore. As you step into this layer, the first thing you might notice is the darkness. You will probably also find that it's very humid. There are very few plants in this layer of the rainforest because only a small amount of sunlight is able to filter down through the upper layers. Soon, however, you will see that the forest floor is actually teeming with life. Let's find out about the creatures and plants that call this dark and humid layer home.

Decomposers

Almost everything that dies in the rainforest ends up on the forest floor. The fallen leaves and dead animals that end up there become food for an abundance of insects, bacteria, and fungi that help to *decompose*, or break down, these things into soil. Together with the humidity of the forest they make the forest floor an efficient decomposing machine. In fact, an ordinary leaf that would take up to a year to decompose on the floor of a temperate forest near your home could completely decompose and disappear on the floor of a tropical rainforest within six weeks.

Give Me the Dirt

All that is decomposed gives life to other organisms. It becomes soil that provides nutrients for plant life. It becomes food for critters such as worms. How do you think the dirt in your neighborhood is made? It also comes from decomposing plant and animal matter. The decomposition just happens a lot slower than in

the rainforest. You can see the process in action by creating your own container for *compost* or decomposing material.

What You Need

- A grown-up to assist
- Garbage pail (either plastic or metal)
- Drill
- Soil or peat moss
- Grass clippings
- Shredded newspapers
- Water
- Shovel

What You Do

1. Ask a grown-up to drill many large holes all around the pail. This will allow air to get into the compost. The bacteria and fungi that will be working to break down the matter into soil need the oxygen from the air just as we do.

2. Place a layer of soil or peat moss in the bottom of the pail. Sprinkle with water.

3. Next, add a layer of grass clippings or shredded newspaper. Water. Repeat the layers until you have filled the container at least halfway.

4. Stir the contents of the pail about every two weeks. Add enough water periodically so that the layers do not dry out. Keeping the layers moist will make the container like the forest floor. It will also keep the container from becoming too smelly. After about a month or two you will have some dark, rich soil to add to your garden.

The Worms Go In and the Worms Go Out

Worms, worms, worms. It seems like worms are everywhere, doesn't it? They really are. Earthworms, the worms that we're most familiar with, belong to a group of worms known as *segmented worms*. There are over 9,000 species of segmented worms in the world, and that is only a fraction of all the worms that are in the world. You probably see the most worms after a rain has drawn them out of the soil. They slither along on driveways and roadways, in puddles and on sidewalks. More worms are in the soil, out of view. There can actually be millions of worms living in your backyard.

Many of the worms in the rainforest do the same thing that the earthworms do in your backyard. They *ingest*, or take in, dirt as they move through the soil and *excrete*, or eliminate, it after it's finely ground in their gizzard and lime from their stomachs is added to it. If

you want to find worms at work, use a stick to poke around moist areas of decaying leaves in the evening. You might catch a worm pulling the leaves into its burrow. The leaves, flowers, and other plant matter that it pulls into its burrow help enrich the soil as these items decay.

Funky Fungi

Have you ever eaten a mushroom? Mushrooms are a type of *fungus*. Fungi are the mega-decomposers of the forest floor. Many mushrooms in the rainforest grow on top of rotting leaves, but there are also other types of fungus that grow in threads among and below them. These threads become like a strong web that feeds on the plant tissue. The threads release a substance that can break down tough plant material. Many fungi live most of their lives underground except for occasionally flowering and fruiting aboveground. Fungi flowers don't look like what you might picture. They are odd-shaped, and most smell awful.

Not all fungi are decomposers. Some of them actually form a mat around the roots of plants that is helpful to the plant. Instead of the fungus killing the plant, the fungus obtains nitrogen and sugars from the plant roots, while the plant absorbs minerals from the fungus. This relationship is called *symbiosis*, which means that both the fungus and the plant benefit from the relationship.

Make a Fern Print T-Shirt

Few plants are able to live on the dark forest floor, and the ones that can are adapted to live in these low-light, humid conditions. Among these few species that can survive among the tree roots, fungi, and decaying matter on the forest floor are ferns and ginger. There are over 12,000 species of ferns in the world, many of which grow in tropical rainforests. Native people of the rainforests often use the beautiful leaves, or *fronds*, of ferns to adorn themselves, adding them to a headdress or wearing them around the neck, as they do in parts of Australia. Here's a way that you can also adorn yourself with ferns.

What You Need

🌾 1 white T-shirt

🌾 Cardboard

🌾 Ferns (available at a local florist)

🌾 Newspaper

🌾 Green fabric paint (available at craft supply stores)

🌾 Paper plate

🌾 Paintbrush

What You Do

1. Wash and dry the T-shirt without using any fabric softener. (Fabric softener hinders the paint from adhering to the fabric.)

2. Place a sheet of cardboard inside the shirt so that the paint does not seep through to the back of the shirt.

3. Place your fern plant on a sheet of newspaper. Tear off one large fern frond close to the dirt. You'll use this to create the fern image on the shirt.

4. Squirt some of the fabric paint onto the paper plate. Paint the fabric paint on the fern. Make sure you have an even coverage of paint on the fern.

5. Lift the fern carefully and turn the painted side down, facing the T-shirt. Carefully lay the fern on the T-shirt and gently press so that all the paint transfers to the fabric.

6. Slowly lift your fern from the T-shirt. Continue creating your fern design by using different sizes of fern fronds on your shirt or reapplying paint to the same fern frond. Allow the paint to completely dry before you remove the cardboard. Voilà—you have your own designer fern T-shirt.

Cook Up Some Fiddleheads

Ferns are not only appreciated for their beauty. They have a variety of important uses. Some ferns are just ornamental, while others are used as food and medicine. Many species of fern found inside and outside of the rainforest can be boiled and eaten. Larger, more substantial fern fronds from the tree ferns of Australia and New Guinea have even been used as splints for people who have a broken limb, and as small fences. You might be able to find the small, curled-up fronds of the ferns called fiddleheads in your grocery store's produce section. These are edible. They are usually available during the spring months.

Here's an easy recipe for fiddleheads that you can try at home.

4 appetizer or side dish servings

What You Need

- 2 cups (473 ml) fresh fiddleheads
- Medium-sized pot filled with water
- Wire whisk
- 1 egg
- 2 bowls
- 1 cup (190 g) flour
- 2 tablespoons (29 g) butter
- Medium-sized sauté pan
- Salt to taste
- A grown-up to assist

What You Do

1. Place the fiddleheads in the pot filled with water. Heat until boiling, then lower the heat and continue to cook the fiddleheads until they are tender (about 5 minutes). When they seem tender, remove the pot from the stove and drain the water from the fiddleheads.

2. Use the wire whisk to beat the egg in one of the bowls until it is frothy. Pour the flour into the other bowl.

3. Place the butter in the sauté pan and heat on medium heat.

4. Dip each tender fiddlehead into the egg, followed by the flour, and then place it in the sauté pan.

5. Ask a grown-up to turn the fiddleheads as they begin to brown. Once brown, they can be removed from the pan. Add salt to taste and enjoy.

Big Bugs

Worms are not the only rainforest inhabitants that make their home on the forest floor. There are beetles, cockroaches, scorpions, and spiders, among others. And these bugs aren't your average garden-variety bugs. The many-legged, wormlike millipedes that you might find in your own garden grow to about an inch long, but in the rainforest their relatives are the largest in the world, growing up to a foot (30 cm) long. The tiny centipedes that you might find living under a log are flatter than millipedes and have one pair of legs for each body segment, unlike millipedes, which have two pairs of legs per segment. In the rainforest carnivorous centipedes grow up to six inches (15 cm) long, and they feed on small animals and other insects using a pair of poisonous claws to catch their prey.

Most scorpions prefer hot, dry deserts, but not all. The Philippine scorpion prefers the humid rainforest floor. It spends its days in burrows and comes out at night to feed on insects.

The largest spider in the world lives in the rainforests of South America. This is the tarantula. The bird-eating spider living in South America, *Theraphosa blondi*, is a member of the tarantula family. This spider would surely frighten Little Miss Muffet, for this is no eensy-weensy spider! Its large 3½-inch (9 cm) body is surrounded by eight 10-inch (25 cm) legs, which makes it the largest spider in the world. Use a ruler to imagine how large the spider actually is. Tarantulas spin a strand of silk to act as a trip wire to alert them to their prey. Once something has tripped the line of silk, the tarantula leaps out, bites its victim, and swallows it whole.

You can visit your local pet store to see live tarantulas. The ones that you will see in the pet shop are a bit smaller than the *Theraphosa blondi*, but still a lot larger than your average house spiders.

Rainforest millipedes grow up to a foot long.

Tarantula

Spy on a Spider

Many species of spiders live in rainforests. Some are even the same as the ones that live in your area. Spiders are not insects. Insects have six legs, while spiders have eight. Spiders have only two major body segments—the head and the thorax are one segment, and the abdomen is the other. Insects have three separate segments—head, thorax, and abdomen. The last thing that separates spiders from insects is that spiders do not have antennae.

Use this activity to take a closer look at the spiders that inhabit your part of the country.

What You Need

- Clear glass jar
- Some sticks
- A piece of a stocking that will fit over the top of the jar
- Rubber band
- Magnifying glass

What You Do

1. Start by searching out some spiders and spiderwebs. Look in the corners of your house and in your garden.

2. When you locate a spiderweb, examine it. There are many different types of webs, but the most common one that you will find is an orb (circular) web.

3. After you have examined the spiderweb, see if you can locate the spider. Knock it gently into your jar using a stick. Never touch the spider with your hands. As soon as the spider is inside the jar, add a few sticks to the jar and cover the jar opening with the piece of stocking. Secure it with a rubber band.

4. Look at your spider. Count its legs. Does it have eight? Spiders have eight eyes. Use the magnifying glass against the jar to see if you can see the spider's eyes. Spend some time watching your spider. It might try to spin a web around the sticks in the jar. Don't keep your spider in the jar for longer than one day because it will need food and water.

5. After completing your examinations, return the spider to the place you found it.

Anansi

The Anansi tales began with the Ashanti people of the rainforest country of Ghana, on the west coast of Africa. *Anansi* means "spider" in the Ashanti language. The Anansi, or spider, in the tales is sometimes wise, other times foolish, often amusing, and at times lazy. In any case, Anansi always teaches a lesson. The Anansi tales traveled with Africans to the Caribbean islands and the United States, where they are still told. Here's a version of the tale of how Anansi acquired all of the stories from Nyame, the sky god.

In the beginning, all the tales in Africa and beyond belonged to the Sky God, Nyame. Kwaku Anansi, the spider, wanted more than anything to own these tales himself. And so Anansi wove a web, climbed up to Nyame, and offered to buy the tales. When Nyame saw the small spider climbing his way to the sky he laughed at the thought of Anansi paying the price of the tales.

Nyame looked upon Anansi and said, "The tales come at a great price, Spider. You will have to bring me Onini, the great python; Osebo, the leopard; and Mmoboro, the hornets. This is the price of the tales. Can you do that, Anansi?"

"I can, great Nyame," replied Anansi. And so Anansi climbed down the web and set out to capture the first creature, the great python, Onini. He first went into the forest and cut a
long pole of bamboo and some vines. Then he carried them to the place where Onini made his home. Anansi held the bamboo pole and started talking loudly to himself, "I'm sure this is longer than he. I know it must be so. My wife is wrong."

Onini heard this talk and asked the spider, "What are you talking about to yourself, Anansi?"

"It is my wife. She says this pole is longer than you and stronger. I disagree, Onini."

"Well, Anansi, that is an easy thing to test. Bring the pole here and I will stretch out alongside it. I'm sure you are right," said Onini.

As soon as the great python stretched his body alongside the pole, Anansi quickly wound them both together with the vine. "I have tricked you, Onini, and now I must bring you to Nyame." Anansi wove a web to carry the python to the Sky God. When he saw Onini and Anansi, Nyame simply said, "A price still remains."

Rainforest Reflection

In some rainforest cultures of South America tarantulas are roasted and eaten. They are claimed to have a nutty flavor. Yum!

Anansi quickly set out to capture Mmoboro, the hornets. He first found a gourd and cut a small hole in it. Then he took some water from the river and sprinkled it on himself and the gourd. He found the hornets all around the tree where their nest was and sprinkled some water on them as well. "It's raining," he said to them as he picked up a leaf and held it over his head. "Don't you see me standing here under this leaf for protection? Come into this gourd so the rain will not wet your wings." And so the hornets all flew into the small hole that Anansi had made in the gourd. Once they were all inside the gourd, Anansi wove a strong web over the hole so that they could not escape. "I have tricked you, Mmoboro, and now I must bring you to Nyame."

Anansi wove a web to carry the hornets to the Sky God. When he saw Mmoboro and Anansi, Nyame simply said, "A price still remains."

Anansi returned to the forest and quickly set out to capture Osebo, the leopard. The leopard was quite large and not easily tricked, so Anansi thought long and hard. He followed the leopard's tracks and then dug a deep pit in the ground, which he covered up with sticks and leaves. The next day Anansi set out to look at the pit. Sure enough, the leopard was found lying in the bottom of it. "I have tricked you, Osebo, and now I must bring you to Nyame." Of course, the leopard was harder to manage than the others, and Anansi found he needed to weave a web very quickly to secure the large animal.

When he arrived in front of the Sky God with the last creature, Nyame had to concede that Anansi had done what no others had been able to do. Nyame gave all the tales to Anansi, and that is why today we call these "Spider Tales." Anansi returned to the forest, and he and his wife set out to learn all of the tales. The spiders never stopped weaving the great tales, for everywhere you look you can see their beautiful webs.

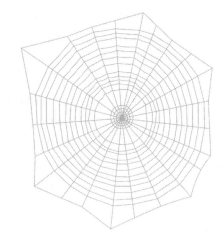

Looking Up

It's time to explore the next layer of the rainforest. It's easy to find. Just look up, but not too far. The next layer is called the *understory*.

2

THE UNDERSTORY

If you look up as you are standing on the forest floor of a tropical rainforest you will see above you and around you an enormous variety of large green leaves from trees and bushes that reach a height of 10 to 20 feet (3 to 6 m). This layer will seem a bit lighter to you than the forest floor, but not much. Very little sunlight reaches this layer, just as we discovered in Chapter 1 about the forest floor. And while your eyes are filled with the greens of the forest, your ears will fill with the very loud, nonstop sounds of insects and birds. Are you ready for an adventure? Then off to the green understory layer of the tropical rainforest we go!

Calabash tree

It flies off to another flower and the pollen falls off onto this flower. Bees are terrific pollinators. Although there are many insects in the rainforest, pollination is sometimes a problem because the flowers can be difficult to see among all of the green in the understory. Some trees have overcome this problem by producing very large, white, strong-smelling flowers that grow on their trunks and bloom at night.

Let's examine the traits that make the flowers successful at attracting insects. First of all, they are large, which really helps them to be seen. It's easy to see a large, white flower at night against a dark jungle of plants. Second, they stink. "Strong smelling" is an understatement for many of these flowers. They can be very stinky! The stink helps attracts moths to the flowers at night. Moths help pollinate the flowers at night, just as bees do during the day. The third and final trait is that many of these flowers grow on the trunks of the plants rather than on stems. How do you think this helps? Read on to find out.

The Not-So-Sweet-Smelling Understory Flowers

Flowers need insects to pollinate them so that they can reproduce. *Pollination* happens when an insect lands on a flower and inadvertently picks up pollen on its legs.

Cauliflower or Cauliflory?

These two words sound very similar, but mean very different things. Both words can be broken down from the Latin *caulis*, meaning stem, to mean "stem-flowering." You have probably heard of or eaten cauliflower, the crunchy vegetable with the underdevel-oped flower and large head that is related to broccoli. *Cauliflory*, on the other hand, is the term used for flowers and fruits that sprout from tree trunks and large branches in tropical rainforests. The redbud and cacao are two examples of tree trunks that sprout such foliage. Many of these flowers and fruits are quite large; so large, in fact, that a branch might not be able to hold them up. The large branches and tree trunks are much stronger and better at supporting these large flowers and fruits.

Houseplant Trading Cards

Many of the plants that we consider houseplants grow wild and thrive in the understory level of tropical rain-forests. Because they receive only a small amount of direct sunlight or rainfall at this level, they adapt easily to the conditions inside a house, where the light is also filtered. Here's your chance to explore the jungle plants that have adapted to life in your house. While you're at it, create these trading cards with your friends to share and swap.

What You Need

- Houseplants
- Plants Found in Tropical Rainforests table (next page)
- Large telephone book or a book of similar size
- Index cards (4 x 6 inches or 10.16 x 15.24 cm)
- Pencil
- Clear contact paper (1 roll)
- Scissors
- Shoe box

What You Do

1. Search your house for houseplants. See if the name of each plant is on an identifying card stuck into the dirt. If not, use the house plant guide on the next page.

2. Get permission to pick one leaf from each houseplant, and then pick them.

3. Look at each leaf. You will probably see that the upper side of the leaf is darker than the underside. That is because there are more cells that contain *chlorophyll* on the top of the leaf. The chlorophyll helps catch the sunlight to make food for the plant through the process of *photosynthesis*, which transforms sunlight into simple sugars for the plant. What shape is your leaf? See if you can draw it.

4. Place each leaf between the pages of the phone book to press them. Use the pages toward the end of the book. Place some extra weight on top of the book and set the book aside for at least a week.

PLANTS FOUND IN TROPICAL RAINFORESTS

Plant Name	Origin	Plant Name	Origin
African Violet	Eastern Africa	Pachypodium	Madagascar
African Lily	Southern Africa	Peace Lily	Tropical America
Aloe	Madagascar	Philodendron	Tropical America
Anthurium	Mexico	Portulacaria (Elephant Bush)	Africa
Asparagus Fern	Southern Africa	Protea	Southern Africa
Caladium	Brazil	Purple Passion	Tropical Asia
Calla Lily, Arum Lily, or Pig Lily	Southern Africa	Sansevieria (Snake Plant)	Madagascar, Southern Africa, Arabia
Canary Islands Ivy	Canary Islands		
Chinese Evergreen	Malaysia	Schefflera	Australia
Colocasia (Elephant's Ear)	Tropical Asia	Scilla Violacea (Silver Squill)	Eurasia, Africa
Dracaena	Africa	Spider Plant	Southern Africa
Ficus (Weeping Fig)	India	Staghorn Fern	Southern Africa
Kalanchoe	Madagascar	Streptocarpus (Cape Primrose)	South Africa, Madagascar
Mimosa Pudica (Sensitive Plant)	Tropical America	Wax Plant	Tropical Asia

5. After the leaves are completely pressed, carefully take them out of the phone book and place each one on an index card. Write the plant name on each card.

6. Look at the table (on the previous page) and see if you can find the rainforest origin of your plant. If it is listed, include that information on your card.

7. Next, add any other information about each plant that you want to include. You might want to add measurements, care instructions, and flowering information.

8. When you have completed your card, place it on top of a piece of contact paper that covers the bottom of the card. Place another piece of contact paper on the top of the card and press down firmly with your hands. Try to avoid capturing any air bubbles under the contact paper. This process will preserve the leaves so they will maintain their color and stay intact for years to come.

9. Use scissors to trim the contact paper around the card. Now your card is ready to share or swap with a friend.

10. Stash your cards in an empty shoe box.

Rainforest Reflection

Try to picture each plant growing wild in the understory of the rainforest. Look in the Rainforest Resources section for Web sites that have photographs of these plants in the wild.

Rainforest Bottle Terrarium

Here's a way to create your own miniature rainforest environment with the same houseplants you used in the trading cards activity. Your finished rainforest terrarium will last about a year.

What You Need

- 2-liter clear plastic soda bottle (opaque bottom)
- A grown-up to assist
- Craft knife
- Gravel or small stones
- Charcoal
- Potting soil
- Small plants (try philodendron and other tropical plants)
- Water

What You Do

1. Soak the bottle in some soapy water and peel off the label. Wash out the inside of the bottle as well.

2. Ask a grown-up to remove the bottom base of the soda bottle with the craft knife and set it aside. Next, ask the grown-up to cut away the top of the bottle at the point where the bottle starts to slope to the opening. You will then have the dome to fit on your terrarium.

3. Check to make sure your base does not have any holes. If it does, place a coffee filter or some large stones inside it to prevent the soil from coming out of the holes.

4. Add some gravel or small stones to the base to help with drainage. Spread about an inch of charcoal over the gravel.

5. Fill the base with the potting soil and begin planting your houseplants in the potting soil. Poke a hole for each plant, set the plant in the hole, and cover the hole with soil. Try to mix plants of different heights.

6. After you've planted all of the plants, water them with about ⅓ cup (79 ml) of water. Take the soda bottle top and invert it on top of the base. Press down until the bottle is firmly attached to the base.

7. Place your miniature rainforest in an area with indirect light. It should not need any more watering. Watch as water droplets, called *condensation*, rain down on your plants from the dome of the terrarium. This condensation will keep your plants from needing to be watered. Your terrarium will be very similar to the tropical rainforest environment.

Sensational Sounds

When you venture into the woods, you often hear the sounds of birds and maybe a rustle of leaves, but for the most part the temperate rainforests of the United States are quiet. They are places where people often go to meditate and find serenity. Not so in the tropical rainforest. There is no such thing as quiet in the jungle. In fact, the greatest concentration of sound-producing insects is usually in the understory layer. Birds, insects, frogs, mammals, and other critters are so abundant in the rainforest that it is impossible to have any quiet. And they don't stop when the sun goes down. Many creatures are active at night in the rainforest, so the sounds of critters are heard even in the dark. And you thought crickets were loud on camping trips!

You can listen to some of the sounds of the rainforest on the Web sites listed under Chapter 2 in the Rainforest Resources section. Close your eyes while you listen to the sounds and try to imagine that you are in the jungle. Think about the different creatures you are hearing. Can you separate the different sounds? How many different creatures do you think you hear? Think about what the creatures are doing when they are making these sounds. Can you picture any of them in your mind?

Snakes Slither in the Understory

The anaconda, the boa constrictor, the very venomous Fer-de-lance snake, and other snakes are quite comfortable in the understory of the rainforest, however, you might never see one on a rainforest visit. These snakes are not as abundant as you might think, and they don't drop from trees as you might see in a movie. Some of these snakes, such as the anaconda, hunt during the day, but are most active at night. Even if they are not seen, however, these snakes are present and are strong predators in the rainforest food chain.

If you did encounter a snake in the rainforest, you would certainly admire its beauty. The emerald tree boa, for example, is as brilliant as the jewel it is named after. Check the Rainforest Resources section for information on photographs of rainforest snakes on the Internet.

Emerald Tree Boa

record measured close to 40 feet (12 m) long, but there are stories of anacondas measuring up to 140 feet (42 m) long. Not only is the anaconda a long snake, it can weigh up to 500 pounds (227 kg). Can you imagine a snake that large? Here's a way to compare its size with yours.

Sizing Up Rainforest Snakes

The largest snake in the world lives in the Amazon rainforest. It is the anaconda. The largest anaconda on

What You Need

- Tape measure
- Ball of yarn
- Scissors
- Scale

1. Use the tape measure to measure out 40 feet (13 m) of yarn. Cut the length from the ball.

2. Stretch out the length of yarn out in an open area outside. It is certainly long, isn't it?

3. Lie down next to the yarn. How many kids do you think it would take to reach 40 feet? Now, can you imagine an anaconda that long? If it stood on end it would be about as tall as a four-story building!

4. Weigh yourself on the scale. An anaconda can weigh 500 pounds (227 kg). How much more does the anaconda weigh than you weigh? See if you can find out what might weigh as much as an anaconda.

Draw the Wowla

The boa constrictor is known as a *wowla* in the country of Belize. It is related to the python, another *constrictor*. Constrictors come in a variety of sizes, and they all kill their prey by wrapping around and suffocating it. All snakes swallow their prey whole, and constrictors are no exception. A large constrictor can consume a whole antelope and then go for as long as two years without another meal.

Look at the book *The Little Prince* by Antoine de Saint-Exupéry. In the first few pages the author describes the way boa constrictors eat. That description is accompanied by two drawings of a boa constrictor digesting an elephant. Try drawing your own Drawing Number One and Drawing Number Two, just as Antoine de Saint-Exupéry did in his classic story.

What You Need

🜲 *The Little Prince* by Antoine de Saint-Exupéry

🜲 Paper

🜲 Crayons

What You Do

1. For Drawing Number One, draw the shape of the snake with an animal inside it, just as Saint-Exupéry did. Elephants are a bit large for a boa constrictor to really swallow, so picture an animal other than an elephant inside of the boa.

You shouldn't see the animal in your finished picture, just the bulge in the boa where the animal is inside.

2. For Drawing Number Two, show the animal inside of the snake. This is sort of like an X-ray picture. Here's a tip: draw the animal first, then draw the outline of the snake around the animal.

3. Show your Drawing Number One to a grown-up or some friends. Can they guess what animal is inside your snake? Make sure you show them Drawing Number Two afterward.

Rainforest Reflection

Peter, Paul, and Mary, a musical group, sang a song about a boa. The song, simply titled "Boa Constrictor," starts off with "I'm being swallowed by a boa constrictor . . . " and then names all the parts of the body that the boa is swallowing. Make up your own song about a hungry boa to the tune of "Ring Around the Rosy." Look in the Rainforest Resources section for more information about the song "Boa Constrictor."

Onward and Upward

If you could see past the understory leaves you would see that the rainforest continues climbing into the sky. In fact, there are two more layers above the understory. You'll need some serious climbing gear to explore these, or you can just turn to Chapter 3 to reach the next layer.

THE CANOPY

Entering the primary layer of the rainforest, which rises to 150 feet (46 m), you'll find trees with smooth, oval leaves, and plenty of fruits, nuts, flowers, and plants that seem to grow out of the air. This layer, called the *canopy*, is so thick that the sunlight that shines down upon it has a very difficult time filtering through to the understory and forest floor below. That is why this layer is often referred to as the *umbrella*. The crowns of the trees fill in gaps around the larger tree crowns that are in the uppermost layer above the canopy, forming an umbrella that catches the rainfall and absorbs sunlight.

To really examine the canopy you have to climb up and up and onto one of the man-made walkways that have been built in the rainforest for exploration. From this vantage point you can walk between trees, from the crown of one to the crown of another. The tops of the trees sway back and forth. That and the height can make the walk terrifying, but it's like no other experience.

Fruits, Flowers, and Nuts

The canopy is the hub of photosynthesis. The wide, green leaves of the canopy trees are able to take in a lot of sunlight. With all this energy the trees are then able to produce many fruits, flowers, and nuts. All of these bring many more colors to this layer. Hummingbirds and other species of birds, bats, and insects work at pollinating the flowers at this level. Step into the produce aisle of your grocery store and you will see many of the fruits and nuts that grow in the rainforest canopy. Mangoes, papayas, bananas, and guavas come from the canopy. You'd also see cashews and Brazil nuts growing there.

Make Rainforest GORP

Do you know what GORP stands for? GORP is an *acronym*, meaning that each letter stands for a word. In this case, the letters GORP stand for "Good Old Raisins and Peanuts." The main ingredients in traditional GORP used for hiking trips are raisins and peanuts, which provide hikers with energy. But GORP can consist of an assortment of fruit, nuts, and snack foods. This rainforest GORP uses some exotic ingredients found in the rainforest canopy. Make some for your next hike and take along this taste of the rainforest.

2–3 servings

What You Need
- Measuring cup
- ¼ cup (20 g) cashews
- ¼ cup (20 g) coconut flakes
- ¼ cup (20 g) banana chips
- ½ cup (40 g) dried papaya
- ½ cup (40 g) dried mango
- ½ cup (40 g) chocolate chips
- Mixing bowl
- Spoon
- Resealable plastic bags

What You Do

1. Measure out the quantities of each ingredient and pour them into the mixing bowl.

2. Mix together.

3. Spoon the mixture into the plastic bags. Take your GORP with you on your next hike or pack some into your lunch bag and enjoy the tastes of the rainforest wherever you go.

What other words can GORP stand for? How about "Great Old Rainforest Pieces"? Can you come up with your own words that represent your rainforest GORP?

Canopy Ponds

Way up high in the rainforest canopy in South American rainforests are a group of tropical plants called *bromeliads*. Bromeliad plants have firm, waxy leaves that grow in a circular cluster. Many of these plants are *epiphytic*, meaning that they grow on other plants without harming them, and not on the ground. They are often called "air plants" because they seem to be rooted in the air and not in the earth. These plants have a terrific way to get water high above the earth. Their leaves, which tend to be long and curved, overlap at the base. When rain falls in the forest, water falls right into the center of the plant. A nice little tank or mini-pond is formed, upon which many other creatures rely to live. (Look in the Rainforest Resources section for information on purchasing a bromeliad to grow at home.)

Bromeliad growing on a tree

Create a Pineapple Pond

Bromeliads belong to the pineapple family called *Bromeliacea*. Although pineapples do not actually grow in the rainforest, they have many of the same characteristics as rainforest plants. What better way to explore bromeliads than to grow your own pineapple right at home!

What You Need

🦟 A grown-up to assist

🦟 Kitchen knife

🦟 Fresh pineapple with healthy green leaves

🦟 Potting soil

🦟 Container that will fit the pineapple base

🦟 Shovel

Rainforest Reflection

Have you ever visited the southern United States and seen the grayish-green Spanish moss that hangs from the trees? It's actually not a true moss at all. Spanish moss is epiphytic, which means that it relies on another plant for support. Surprisingly, it's also a member of the pineapple family.

What You Do

1. Ask a grown-up to cut off the top of your pineapple, making sure to leave 2 to 3 inches (5 to 8 cm) of the fruit attached to the pineapple leaves on top.

2. Allow the pineapple to dry for a day or two. When it is dry, scrape away the soft fruit, leaving the pineapple center, or core, attached to the leaves.

3. Your pineapple is now ready to plant. Add the soil to your container. Place the pineapple base onto the soil. Shovel some soil onto the base, making sure the leaves are not covered by the soil. Tap the soil down firmly.

4. Place your pineapple in a sunny window. Water the plant when the soil becomes dry.

5. Your pineapple will begin to develop new leaves. In the summer, place your plant outside in a sheltered area that does not get full sun. Leave the plant outside for at least a week, making sure to water it if it doesn't rain.

6. Look at your pineapple regularly and see what you find in the center of the leaves. Does water collect there after it rains? If so, you can see how the bromeliads in the rainforest also collect water. Imagine very large plants with many living creatures living in the plant's very own pond.

Note: It takes about two years for a pineapple plant to grow fruit. If after two years your plant has not flowered and grown a fruit, you can force it to flower by placing it in a plastic bag with an apple. After three to four days a red cone will appear, then blue flowers. After six months the plant will fruit.

Draw Who Lives in the Pond

Many creatures make their home in the canopy bromeliads. In fact, a bromeliad tank or pond, which can hold anywhere from a cup (237 ml) to 12 gallons (45 l) of water (and sometimes even more!), can support an entire ecosystem or community. Inside the water you can often find frog tadpoles, crabs, mosquito larvae, and other insect eggs. Salamanders, snails, frogs, and a host of insects live around the pond. Even monkeys and animals such as the mouse opossum come to the tank for water to drink.

Create this paper bromeliad to show all the creatures that can live in the pond of one bromeliad.

What You Need

❊ Scissors

❊ 3 or more sheets of green paper (8½ × 11 inches or 21.59 × 27.94 cm)

❊ Clear tape

❊ Markers

What You Do

1. Cut a strip of green paper about 4 inches by 8½ inches (10.16 by 21.59 cm) long. Tape the ends together to form a tube that is 4 inches (10.16 cm) high. That will form the pond or tank of the bromeliad.

2. Cut the remainder of the green sheet in half lengthwise and in half again to create 4 strips. Use the scissors to cut a pointed end on each strip. Your finished strips will form the inside leaves of your bromeliad.

3. Tape each leaf to the outside of the bromeliad pond circle so that they hang outside.

4. Cut each remaining sheet of paper into three long strips that are each 11 inches (27.94 cm) long. Use your scissors to cut one end of each strip into a point to form the leaves.

5. Continue taping the leaves around the pond, overlapping the leaves as you go around. When you have finished taping all the leaves around the pond, use your hands to fold the leaves back. The leaves become layered and end up looking similar to those of a pineapple.

6. Use markers to decorate your bromeliad by drawing all of the creatures that live in it on the leaves. Remember to hide some underneath the leaves, just like a real rainforest bromeliad.

7. Show your bromeliad to your friends. Can they find all of the creatures you drew inside?

The Orchids

Have you ever seen an orchid? This beautiful flower comes in all sorts of colors ranging from white to pink to deep violet to orange and even yellow. Their bright colors make orchids stand out to pollinating insects in rainforest jungles. There are about 20,000 different species of orchids—the second largest variety for a flowering plant (the plant that has the most is the sunflower). You can find orchids in most flower shops. They symbolize love, beauty, wisdom, and thoughtfulness. Cut orchid flowers can last for a long time, usually 7 to 10 days in a vase, making them a very desirable cut flower. In the wild rainforests, the flowers may bloom for months at a time.

About half of all the orchid species are epiphytic. They spread their thick, white roots over the surface of the bark of the trees that give them support. Since they are high up in the canopy, you might wonder where these orchids get water to survive. Orchid plants have roots that enable them to take up water quickly when it rains. When the rain is gone, the thick leaves retain the water for the plant until the next rain. Orchids grow in many rainforests around the world, but Asian rainforests seem to have the richest variety of these beautiful plants. The earliest history of orchids was written in China and Japan 4,000 years ago!

Rainforest Reflection

Hawaiian *leis*, or flower necklaces, made of orchids have symbolized love, friendship, and joy for centuries. Turn to Chapter 8 to learn how to make your own.

Play the Orchid Game

Orchids have unique colors, scents, and shapes that are meant to attract pollinating insects. Some, like the slipper orchid, have petals that are shaped to attract insects. The petals guide the bee or fly to the center of the flower, where it is slippery. The insect then falls into the flower and must crawl out past the pollen sacs and stamens to get out. Other orchids use bright, showy colors or strong scents to attract insects.

Play this game with a group of friends to find out how important the tool of color is to rainforest orchids.

What You Need

- Crepe paper in assorted colors, including bright pink, jungle green, and white
- Scissors
- Bandanna
- Paper
- Pencil
- 15 or more friends

WHAT YOU DO

1. Put the crepe paper on a table with a pair of scissors. Have five friends leave the room with the bandanna.

2. Everyone else should begin decorating him- or herself with pieces of crepe paper. Cut and tie strips around your arms and body. Make a headband using different colors.

3. After everyone is finished, stand together in a group in the center of the room. Have one of the friends from outside the room come back in, blindfolded with the bandanna.

4. On the count of three, have the friend remove the blindfold and look at the group. Which three people does the friend notice first? Write their names down.

5. Have each of the other friends who were sent out of the room come back in, one at a time, blindfolded, to do the same thing.

6. Look at the lists of friends who were noticed first. Are the same names on all the lists? Do they have anything in common? What colors did they choose?

7. Think about a bee that is in the rainforest. Which flowers do you think it will notice first? What are some other ways that plants attract insects?

A World on a Tree Branch

Just as there are layers in the rainforest, there are also layers on the tree branches of the canopy. If you looked at a tree branch in the rainforest you would find that it has a layer of soil, which comes from windborne dust, fallen leaves, animal droppings, and plant and animal remains. Ants and other insects live in this

layer. Mosses, lichens, and some epiphytes make up the second layer of the branch. The next layer is made up of bromeliads, ferns, orchids, and many other plants. In fact, sometimes small trees grow out from the center of bromeliads in this layer. The last layer is filled with the animals of the canopy. Depending on the location of the rainforest, these animals may include frogs, butterflies, snakes, birds, and mammals. One thing that is certain—insects abound in all the layers of all rainforests.

Canopy Climbers

It takes a certain kind of scientist to study the rainforest canopy—certainly one who isn't afraid of heights! These scientists risk their lives climbing into the unexplored world at the top of the trees. How do they get up there? Some use climbing ropes, while others use structures that provide a staircase to the top. Cranes, booms, and gondolas have also been used. When atop, scientists find insects and other creatures that have never been seen before. They have found that a single tree in the Amazon rainforest can yield more than three pounds (1.36 kg) and more than 1,700 different species of insects and other creatures. Amazing, isn't it?

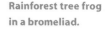

Rainforest tree frog in a bromeliad.

Going Up!

There is one more layer at the very top of the rainforest. You probably thought this was it. Not quite. Rainforest trees grow even higher, right up into the sky! You'll find out just how high in the next chapter.

4
AT THE TOP

Finally, we are at the top of the rainforest. Looking down from this layer you see a sea of green and looking up you see just blue sky. The tall trees that reach this layer appear like islands in the green sea. They poke out and upward toward the sky. This is the world of toucans and other brightly colored birds that fly from island to island. But birds aren't the only ones flying here. There are also blue morpho butterflies and other insects. Let's take a closer look at these tall trees, known as *emergents*, from the ground level on up toward the sky, and at the creatures that also call this layer home.

From Lowly Beginnings

The giant emergent trees, which can be anywhere from 200 to 800 years old, make their start like other rainforest trees, in the soil of the dark forest floor. They begin with a simple seed that is carried on the wind and brought to a spot on the forest floor. The seedling begins to grow. It will do best if it's in a *clearing,* or gap in the canopy. The leaves of these seedlings are not the same as the leaves they will have when they're fully grown. As the plant grows and begins to reach above the canopy, its leaves become smaller and tougher. These will help the young plant survive and thrive in the heavy sunshine and wind at the top. The leaves also develop a waxy layer that helps them retain moisture in this drier atmosphere.

Compare Buildings and Buttresses

It takes a lot to support a tree that may reach 200 or more feet into the air. If that tree were planted in a city, it would stand shoulder to shoulder with a 20-story building. That is very tall! The wind that these trees encounter at that height is 100 times greater than the trees in the understory, and about 10 to 20 times greater than those in the canopy. In order to stand strong against the wind, the trees at this height must adapt. One adaptation is the formation of *buttresses,* which look like wings that spread out from the base of the tree. In part one of this activity, see if you can create your own buttresses that demonstrate how the buttresses of the emergent trees work. Then try your hand at part two, and learn how these rainforest trees have inspired architecture.

PART ONE

What You Need

🪰 Clay

What You Do

1. Take a ball of clay that is a little larger than your hand and begin to roll it out to form a long snake that is about ½ inch (1.27 cm) thick and about 12 inches (30.48 cm) long. This will form your tree trunk.

2. Try to stand your tree trunk up on a flat surface. Does it stand up? Create a gust of wind by blowing on it. Does it stand up?

3. Take another ball of clay and begin to shape some buttresses, or wings. Make them about ¼ inch (.64 cm) thick, and press them into the sides of the base of your tree. The buttresses should begin at the very bottom of the tree and continue about one-fourth of the way up the trunk of your tree. Look at the picture of the tree here to get an idea of how the buttresses form the base of the tree. You might need someone to help hold your tree up while you add the buttresses around the tree.

4. Now pull your hands away. Can your tree stand up now? How well do you think the buttresses work?

PART TWO

Architecture is often inspired by nature. How do buttresses fit in with buildings? Well, tall towers are constructed with thicker bases. As they get taller they also get thinner. The extra weight at the base keeps them firmly supported. Try this experiment with your friends to test the support of buttresses.

What You Need

🪰 12 friends

What You Do

1. Have one friend get down on the floor on all fours. Have another try to balance on the back of the first, and a third attempt to balance on the back of the second. Does it work? Can you build a tower with one person on the base?

2. Try having three people line up side by side on all fours. Have two people try to balance on the backs of the three, and another climb up to form a pyramid. Does it work with a larger base?

3. Experiment with different numbers on each level. What works best? Try this same experiment with blocks. What is the best way to build the tallest tower? Have a contest with your friends to see who can build the tallest tower.

Amazon toucan

On the Wing

Brightly colored birds take to the air, flying from one emergent tree to another. Macaws, toucans, hawks, eagles, and other birds have brilliantly colored feathers that do anything but *camouflage* (hide) them among the green of the forest. For example, the scarlet macaw is one of the most spectacular parrots of South America. It not only is feathered in bright scarlet, as its name describes, but also boasts brilliant blue and yellow feathers on its wings. Scarlet macaws don't need to be camouflaged because they have very few predators.

The birds of the jungle tend to have short, broad wings. This helps them maneuver the thick vegetation in the rainforest. Some birds have also adapted to climbing. Toucans and parrots are just a few of the species of birds that have feet with toes that can grasp the trunks and branches of trees.

Design a Bird Mask

Many different rainforest cultures create bird masks for special ceremonies and use feathers to adorn themselves. The Highland tribes of the Pacific island of New Guinea decorate wigs with bird of paradise feathers. Chiefs of the ancient Hawaiian islands wore helmets decorated with red, black, and yellow feathers. The red feathers came from the 'I'iwi bird. Along with the yellow feathers, they signified nobility. New Zealand Maori chiefs also decorated themselves with feathers. They wore white-tipped black feathers from the Huia bird. Natives of India, Borneo, and the Philippines incorporated the white, black, and grey feathers of hornbills, relatives of the toucan, into their headdresses. South American Aztecs chose to decorate themselves with brilliant hummingbird feathers. Not all these birds were killed for their feathers. Often the feathers were gathered from molting birds as they shed their feathers each year.

Here's a great bird mask that you can create to adorn yourself. Wear your mask for Carnival, as revelers do in Brazil and other countries right before the Christian period of Lent; for Mardi Gras, which also celebrates the feasting before Lent and is held in New Orleans; for Halloween; or for any other special day you might celebrate.

What You Need

- Scissors
- Foamie sheet (found at craft stores)
- White craft glue
- Basic Halloween eye mask
- Multicolored tissue paper
- Assorted, brightly colored feathers

What You Do

1. Cut the triangular shape of a beak from the foamie sheet. Use the white craft glue to adhere the beak to the nose of the mask. Let the mask dry thoroughly before proceeding.

2. Tear small pieces of tissue paper to use for your mask. Decide which colors you want to use in the design.

3. Spread the glue on the mask with your finger in a nice smooth layer.

4. Start placing pieces of tissue paper on the mask. Let it dry.

5. Turn the mask over and place a line of glue all around the top rim where you will add your feathers.

6. Place the base of your feathers in the glue on the mask. Hold them in place for a minute to make sure the glue holds the feathers.

7. Add any additional feathers to the front of the mask to finish it off. When it's completely dry, try it on and look in a mirror. What's the first thing that pops into your head when you first see the mask? Can you make up a name for your mask character?

Flight into the Heavens

The Indonesian people believe that the souls of people who lived before us take the form of birds in the sky. In New Guinea, it is believed that the bird of paradise escaped from heaven because it is so beautiful and rarely touches the earth. It remains airborne for long periods of time. People of the Amazon believe that the macaw flew to the sun and was punished by the gods for this and given yellow spots. There are many other tales of the beautiful birds of the rainforest. Here is a version of a Mayan tale of the hummingbird. See if this story inspires you to write your own bird tale. Perhaps the bird mask from the previous activity will help inspire you, too.

Rainforest Reflection

The birds of the rainforest make very desirable pets in many countries. In fact, you have probably seen parrots in your local pet store. More than 75 percent of the birds that were captured in the rainforest and sent to the United States and Europe in 1990 were captured in West Africa. For every bird that completed its journey, another 10 died in transit or during the capture. Find out about our current laws on importing birds into the United States. Read more about this problem and how you can help in Chapter 10.

In the beginning—when there was not one bird, one fish, or one mountain—there was sky and there was sea. There were only the two of them and Heart-of-Sky, the creator. He was called Maker, Modeler, Kukulkan, and Hurricane. But there was no one to speak these names. There was no one to praise him or speak of his greatness.

And so he thought, "Who is there to speak my name or give me praise?" And with that, Heart-of-Sky said "earth." As the word was spoken, the earth rose from the sea. He said "sun," and the sun appeared in the sky. Heart-of-Sky then thought of mountains, and the great mountains came. He thought of trees, and the trees grew on the earth. Heart-of-Sky was pleased.

Heart-of-Sky then planned the creatures of the forest, and one by one he created the snakes, jaguars, deer, and birds. When all was finished, he found that he had need for one more bird. So he looked at the feathers and scraps from all the other birds that were created and began to fashion a small bird from those scraps. When the bird was complete it had brilliant colors. The Sun then wanted to help in the creation. And so the Sun added light. They named the bird Tzunu'un, which is the Mayan word for hummingbird.

Heart-of-Sky was so pleased that he created another Tzunu'un and gave the little birds an elaborate wedding feast. The butterflies created a room. Then petals fell from the flowers to create a wonderful carpet. Last, spiders spun silvery webs to create a bridal pathway for the little birds. All the other creatures of the forest attended the wedding. The two little birds were dazzling in the sunshine, but the guests noticed that whenever the groom turned his wings away from the sun, the dazzling colors vanished and he looked drab and gray. The little groom took note of this and so continues to this day to try to stay in the sunlight as he flies through the forests, so that his wings will always be dazzling to his bride.

many of the colors in feathers or skin. For example, the pigment melanin creates the black, brown, gray, and beige colors, while the carotenoid pigments make the red and yellow colors. The other way that color is created in these birds is through the effect of light. These birds have an *iridescence*, or rainbowlike color, created from the arrangement of their feathers. The feathers form slats, just like blinds covering a window, so that the light bounces them and creates the iridescence we see.

The Hummingbird

There are more than 300 hummingbird species in the world. They feed on nectar from flowers and other plants. Rainforest hummingbirds feed on the flowers of the emergent trees, but also fly through clearings into the understory to feed on the flowers below. While hummingbirds are found throughout North and South America, sunbirds, which are very similar and fill the same *niche*, or place, in the rainforest community, live in Africa, Asia, and parts of Australia.

The spectacular colors of hummingbirds and sunbirds are produced in two different ways. As in other creatures, there are pigments or chemicals that create

Build a Hummingbird Feeder Station

The hummingbird that visits your garden in the spring and summer might actually spend its winters in the rainforest trees of Mexico and Central America. Hummingbirds migrate south each winter. Like the robins, they return each spring to the north. Look in the Rainforest Resources section for migration maps to help track your local species of hummingbirds. In the meantime, plan a feeder station for your local hummingbirds to make their stay a happy and successful one.

Rainforest Reflection

Have you ever seen a helicopter? Hummingbirds are natural helicopters. Just like helicopters, they can fly right, left, up, down, backward, even upside down. Watch your feeder carefully. It's easy to miss them. Hummingbirds fly at a speed of about 25 MPH (40 KPH) and small hummingbirds, such as the ruby-throated hummingbird, flap their wings about 55 times per second.

What You Need

- Hummingbird feeder (commercial feeders are best for hummingbirds)
- 4 cups (946 ml) water
- Saucepan
- A grown-up to assist
- 1 cup (224 g) sugar

What to Do

1. Hang your feeder in a sunny spot near some flowers so that the hummingbirds won't have difficulty finding it. Find a spot that gets a few hours of direct sunlight a day and spends the rest of the day in the shade. Try to place it about 10 to 15 feet (3 to 5 m) from a bush or other cover so that the birds will have a safe shelter nearby against harmful weather or cats.

2. Place the water in the saucepan and ask a grown-up to heat the water for you. Before the water comes to a boil, add the sugar. Allow all the sugar to dissolve.

3. Once all the sugar dissolves, turn off the heat and allow the mixture to cool before filling your feeder. Any extra syrup can be stored in the refrigerator for up to two weeks.

4. Keep your feeder clean and filled. Once hummingbirds visit your feeder, they will keep returning throughout the warm months. When the weather turns colder they will migrate south.

Attracting Hummingbirds

Here are some plants that you can add to your garden that will attract hummingbirds:

- Bee Balm
- Columbine
- Azalea
- Beard's Tongue
- Jewelweed
- Salvia
- Butterfly Bush
- Hollyhock
- Foxglove
- Lupine
- Petunia
- Impatiens
- Coral Bells
- Lantana
- Honeysuckle
- Phlox

Look at the flowers of these plants. Can you find any similarities? You will probably see that most flowers are tube-shaped. Their shape is like a cup, from which the hummingbird drinks nectar.

There are many more flowers that also attract hummingbirds. Many plants that attract hummingbirds also attract butterflies. Look at the Plant a Butterfly Garden activity in Chapter 6 for more plants that attract hummingbirds and butterflies.

Into the Jungles

Now that you have explored the four layers of the tropical rainforest, it's time to venture out into the different rainforest jungles. Each one has the same four layers, but you will discover that the animals and plants that live in each are wildly different. The key word is *wildly*.

5
JOURNEY TO AFRICA

What comes to your mind when you think of Africa? Most likely, you think of lions, giraffes, and zebras living in the savannas or grasslands. You wouldn't be wrong, but there is so very much more to the continent of Africa. Think about the jungles you have seen in National Geographic television shows or Tarzan movies—the gorillas, the lizards, and lemurs of Madagascar; and the spices and exotic foods from across the continent. These are the characteristics of the rainforests of Africa.

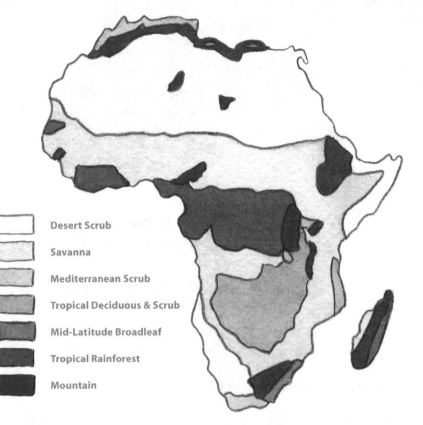

Desert Scrub

Savanna

Mediterranean Scrub

Tropical Deciduous & Scrub

Mid-Latitude Broadleaf

Tropical Rainforest

Mountain

Exploring Africa

The continent of Africa is made up of more than 50 countries and covers nearly 12 million square miles (31 million square km). Deserts and grasslands cover the majority of the land. In fact, only about 10 percent of the continent is forest. Although the most common languages spoken are English, French, Swahili, and Arabic, there are countless others. See what other facts you can find out about the continent of Africa. You might explore the weather of the continent, popular sports there, or the religions of African people.

Mary Kingsley, Jungle Explorer

Rather than preparing for marriage and children, Mary Kingsley was preparing for adventure. Kingsley set out in 1893 for her first expedition to West Africa to collect fish for the British Museum. That trip became one of three that Kingsley took to Africa. She traveled in her long skirts through the swamps of the Congo River and trails of the jungle in search of her specimens. At one point she fell into a pit that was lined with poisoned stakes. Fortunately, Kingsley wasn't seriously

Look at a map of Africa. Can you tell where the rainforests are located? The rainforests and jungles in Africa are located in the middle of the continent, in the countries of the Democratic Republic of the Congo, Cameroon, and Gabon, and on the western coast in the countries of Liberia, Nigeria, Sierra Leone, the Ivory Coast, Ghana, and others. They can also be found on the island of Madagascar, off the southeastern African coast. There are so many wonders to discover. Are you ready for adventure?

hurt and was even heard praising her "good, thick skirt." She collected insects and reptiles along with many fish for the museum. A few previously undiscovered species of fish were named after her, including the *Brycinus kingsleyae* and the *Ctenopoma kingsleyae*.

Mary Kingsley

Kingsley became the authority on West Africa during the nineteenth century after her writings gave people in England and the rest of the world a glimpse into the world of African rainforests. She died while on her third trip to Africa after contracting a fever in South Africa, where she had volunteered as a nurse during the Boer War. One hundred years after her voyages to Africa, a team of biologists went back to explore the fish in the Ogooue River basin in Gabon, as Kingsley had done. Mary Kingsley's work is still a source of inspiration for present-day scientists, and it continues to serve as an important base of knowledge for the regions of Africa she explored.

Rainforest Reflection

Tarzan of the Apes, written by Edgar Rice Burroughs in 1912, was the first look at the rainforest for many Americans. The movie that followed in 1918 wasn't filmed in Africa, though. It was filmed right in the United States, and many animals were brought in to make the jungle look more realistic. Almost a century later, Disney's animated *Tarzan & Jane* introduced a new generation to the tale that Edgar Rice Burroughs wrote so long ago. In this version, Jane and her father travel from their home in England to explore the jungles of Africa, as did many of the early explorers in the late nineteenth and early twentieth centuries.

Record Your Findings in a Jungle Journal

The journals and sketchbooks of the early jungle explorers provided important scientific information for the museums and organizations that sponsored the explorers' expeditions. Their notes and sketches gave details of the rainforest that few people had seen before. Here's how to make your own journal.

What You Need

- Ruler
- Scissors
- Pencil
- Cardboard
- Decorative paper for cover
- Paintbrush
- White craft glue
- White paper
- A grown-up to assist
- Paper hole puncher
- 2½-inch-notebook rings
- Colored pencils

What You Do

1. Measure and cut two 6-inch by 6-inch (15.24 cm by 15.24 cm) squares of cardboard for the covers of your book.

2. Measure and cut two 7-inch by 7-inch (17.78 cm by 17.78 cm) squares of decorative paper. You can use tissue paper, handmade paper, wrapping paper, or wallpaper to decorate the covers of your book.

3. Place the decorative side of your paper face down on a flat surface. Center the cardboard on top of the decorative sheet. Use the scissors to make a tiny slit in each corner of the decorative paper, from the corner of the paper to the corner of the cardboard. Do not cut the cardboard.

4. Lift the cardboard back up and using the paintbrush, spread each decorative sheet with white glue. Place the cardboard back in position on top of the decorative sheet.

5. Use the paintbrush to apply a line of glue to the edges of the cardboard. Then fold the edges of the decorative paper over the cardboard and press firmly. Let the covers dry.

6. Measure and cut several 6-inch by 6-inch (15.24 cm by 15.24 cm) sheets of white paper for the inside pages of your journal.

7. Line up the pages inside of the two covers and ask a grown-up to help punch two holes in your book roughly ¼ inch (.64 cm) from one side.

8. Place a ring in each hole. Now your book is ready for you to record your discoveries. Bring along a pencil to record your findings and some colored pencils for your sketches. The rings will allow you to add more pages as you fill up the book.

Gorillas, Up Close and Personal

Gorillas have often appeared on the big screen, but not always realistically. Gorillas are sometimes seen doing things in the movies that they don't really do in the rainforests of Africa. It is important to be able to separate fact from fiction when you watch movies that take place in the African rainforests (or any rainforest, for that matter). Here's one thing to look for the next time you settle down in front of a movie.

Koko and her kitten

Does the gorilla have a family or is it alone?

- Gorillas in the rainforest *do* live in family groups, usually with one male.
- The family *does* nest each night in the trees upon a platform of branches and leaves that keeps the gorillas off the cold ground while they sleep or keeps them from sliding down a steep slope.

See what else in the movie you can compare to real life in the African rainforests.

Gorilla Talk

Gorillas may not be able to talk as they do in some movies, but there is a gorilla that speaks in American Sign Language. Her name is Koko. Koko is a lowland gorilla. There are two types of gorillas—lowland and mountain. Mountain gorillas live in Congo and Rwanda. They don't move around as much as lowland gorillas, which move around constantly. Lowland gorillas are a little more difficult to see in the rainforest, because even though they move around a lot they tend to stay in the trees. Lowland gorillas are a bit smaller than mountain gorillas.

Koko was born in 1971. When Koko was a baby at the San Francisco Zoo she began a relationship with a young graduate student named Francine "Penny"

Patterson. Together they began the longest continuous language experiment in history. Now, more than 25 years later, Koko can understand spoken English and can speak with 1,000 words in sign language. The Gorilla Language Project that Penny Patterson began has been instrumental in studying gorilla intelligence. It has also given the scientific community a great resource by exploring the world of the gorilla. Presently the Gorilla Foundation that conducts the Gorilla Language Project is working to establish a gorilla preserve on the Hawaiian island of Maui. You can learn more about Koko and plans for the preserve at the Foundation's Web site. See the Rainforest Resources section for the listing.

Gorillas Rediscovered in Nigeria!

For 30 years many believed that western lowland gorillas were extinct in Nigeria. Nigeria, the largest country in West Africa, is home to one in every five Africans. It has a total population of more than 123 million over an area that is a little more than twice the size of California. Compare that to the entire United States population, which is about twice that size at just over 275 million (in 2000). In spite of this dense population, researchers recently discovered that gorillas are still living in Nigeria's forests—possibly up to 300 gorillas living within three to five family groups. This is wonderful news for conservationists. Protection efforts for these gorillas are now underway.

The Mbuti Pygmies

Would you like to live in the rainforest? Where would you shop for food? What would you wear? Would you go to school? People who live in rainforests might laugh at some of these questions because their lives are so different than yours. They might ask different questions about living outside of the jungle. For example, where would I hunt for food? Why do I need shoes? The Mbuti pygmies live in the Ituri rainforest of Zaire in Central Africa. Their lives are intertwined with the health of the jungle. They rely on the rainforest for all their needs, including food, shelter, and clothing.

The Mbuti pygmy men are hunters. They hunt antelope, monkeys, birds, and sometimes elephants. Men also collect honey, which is a prized skill among the pygmies. The women are gatherers. They gather nuts, berries, mushrooms, and roots to eat. They move their community camps every few weeks or months to take advantage of the food sources of the forest.

The Yam

Many other people make their home in the rainforest countries of West Africa and rely on the foods of the rainforest for their survival. Some of these foods, like monkey, snails, antelope, caterpillars, and termites, might not sound too tasty, but there are a lot of other foods that are a bit more familiar. The Ashanti and Yoruba tribes, along with many other West Africans, eat yams, which are a staple of their diet.

The sweet potato plant is a climbing vine with shiny, heart-shaped leaves that have large stems underground that are called *tubers*. The tuber is the yam that

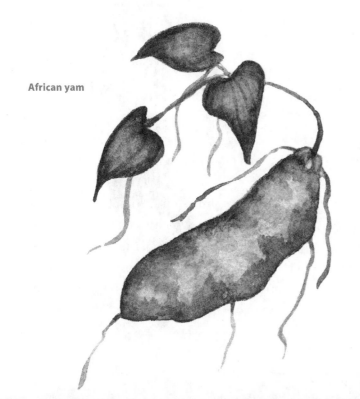

African yam

people eat. It is similar in taste to the sweet potatoes that we find in the United States. The yam is so important to their survival that the tribes celebrate the harvest of the yams each year with a festival called the Festival of the Yams, or Feast of the New Yam. Held every year before the harvest begins, it honors the earth goddess and the ancestors of the tribes. Many yam dishes, such as *fufu* and yam soup, are prepared for the celebration. Many of the celebrations include drum and gourd music and dancing.

Cook Fufu

"Fufu" is composed of yam, plantain, or cassava; it is peeled, boiled, pounded and made into balls, which act the part of European potatoes, only it is far more savoury than the vile tuber, which has already potatofied at least one nation, and which no man of taste ever looks, except in some such deep disguise as maitre d'hotel.

—Richard Burton, explorer, from Wanderings in West Africa, 1863

Fufu is a native dish of West Africa. This stiff pudding, made from yams, plantains (in the banana family), or cassava, another starchy vegetable that is similar to the potato and that is a staple of West African diets. It's used to accompany stews, soups, and sauces, just as we might eat bread, biscuits, pita bread, or dumplings. It is also one of the yam dishes made during the yam festival. Traditionally, the ingredients of fufu are boiled over an open pit and then mashed with a mortar and pestle. A *mortar* is a small bowl-shaped container. A *pestle* is a stick that has a rounded bottom and is used to grind spices and foods in the bowl. You don't have to go to those lengths to make your own fufu. Here's a fufu recipe you can try at home.

4 servings

What You Need

- 4 medium-sized yams
- Potato peeler
- Soup pot
- Water
- A grown-up to assist
- Potato masher
- Salt to taste

What You Do

1. Wash and peel the yams. Place them in the pot and add water to cover them.

2. Ask a grown-up to boil the yams for about 30 minutes or until tender. Then drain the water from the pot.

3. Use the potato masher to mash the yams into a paste. Salt to taste.

4. Wet your hands and roll the mashed sweet potatoes into bite-sized balls. Sprinkle them with water to keep them moist.

5. Serve the fufu with soups and stews. To eat the fufu, take one of the balls and make an indentation in it with your thumb. Use the fufu like a scoop to eat the soup or stew.

Note: Look in the Rainforest Resources section for links to recipes for dishes , such as African stew, to try with your fufu.

A mortar and pestle are used to grind fufu.

Make a Yam Festival Gourd Rattle

Drums and rattles are an integral part of West African celebrations. Tribes use plants from the forest to make their instruments. Gourds play an important part for many of these tribes. The gourd is a vegetable that grows on a vine. There are both hard-shell and ornamental gourds. The bottle gourd is one of the most widely used gourds. In fact, the remains of gourds found in Peru date all the way back to 10,000 B.C. Most gourds used today are cultivated on farms, although many wild ancestors of these gourds have been found in Africa. Botanists believe that the first hard-shelled gourds originated in Africa, and their seeds probably traveled on the seas across to the Americas. Over the centuries, gourds have been used as containers as well as instruments. Here's a simple gourd rattle that you can make, but it takes a long time to finish. For a real challenge, grow your own gourd to use for this project. Look in the Rainforest Resources section for gourd sources.

What You Need
- Bottle gourd (see Rainforest Resources section for mail-order gourds—also available at local farms)
- Liquid detergent
- Warm water
- Scrub brush
- A grown-up to assist
- Capful of bleach
- Rubber gloves
- Acrylic paint

What You Do
1. Soak the gourd in warm, soapy water for about three minutes. This will soften the outer skin so that it will be easier to scrub off.
2. Scrub off the thin outer skin of the gourd using a scrub brush.
3. Ask a grown-up to add the bleach to the scrub water for the last rinsing to eliminate any mold. Use gloves to protect hands from the bleach.
4. Let the gourd dry in a warm room, periodically turning it over, for a few months to a year. When you hear the seeds rattling around inside, your gourd is ready to use.
5. You can now paint your gourd if you like, or leave it natural. Many craftspeople in Ghana cut their gourd at this time and add beads and bells to the inside and then glue it back together to create different sounds to their rattles. Because every gourd is different, every gourd rattle has a different sound. Enjoy yours and make a lot of music!

Africa's Other Rainforest

Off the southeastern coast of Africa lies an island called Madagascar. It is the fourth largest island in the world. Once covered entirely by rainforests, it now has savanna, desert, and prairie areas, as well as the remaining rainforest on the east coast. Africa's *savanna* is sometimes referred to as the bush, because it consists mainly of small bushes, some trees, and grasslands. The *prairie* areas, or *grasslands*, are without trees or bushes. In complete contrast to the African rainforests, the African desert receives extremely little rainfall. In fact, it may get less than 10 inches of rain each year. Some of these drier regions of Madagascar developed because part of the island was used for agriculture and development, and water was sometimes rerouted to farmland. (Learn more about current challenges facing this region by checking out Chapter 10,

and by contacting the rainforest organizations listed in the Rainforest Resources section. You'll be surprised at all of the different ways you can help.) The remaining rainforest in Madagascar has one of the most fascinating and unusual mixes of plants and animals. In fact, there are 66 species of animals that are found only on Madagascar. Boasting an incredible biodiversity, that is, many plant and animal species, Madagascar can claim more than 900 species of orchids, and nine-tenths of the world's lemur species. *Lemurs* are primates, like monkeys, apes, and humans. Madagascar also boasts almost half of the world's reptilian chameleon species.

Madagascar Chameleons

Madagascar's chameleon community is the largest in the world and the most diverse. In addition to the numerous chameleon species found on this island, there are more than 50 that cannot be found anywhere else. Chameleons are nature's quick-change artists. They use the colors of brown, gray, green, yellow, and blue to blend into many different colors. Why do you think they change color? Other creatures, such as the octopus, have the ability to change color, but most of these creatures change color to be camouflaged into their surroundings. The chameleon does not change color to match its surroundings. On the contrary, chameleons quite frequently stand out in their surroundings. Chameleons change color because of light and temperature. They also change color to communicate with other chameleons and potential predators—sort of like a mood ring.

The chameleon actually has a transparent outer skin. Underneath the outer skin are two cell layers that contain red and yellow pigments. Underneath those layers are more cell layers that reflect blue and white light. Another layer is even farther down and contains brown melanin. (*Melanin* is the pigment that gives us our skin color.) When the chameleon is exposed to different amounts of light and heat, or its mood changes to cause internal chemical reactions in these layers, the chameleon changes color. Calm chameleons might be green. When they get angry, they might change to yellow.

Rainforest Reflection
What do you think this old Sufi expression means? "So as the chameleon changes his skin, an unwise one changes the color of his being." Do you agree?

Four-horned chameleon

Mood Ring Challenge

The mood ring, created by Joshua Reynolds, became as popular in the 1970s as the smiley face and the pet rock. The ring has a heat-sensitive crystal and is embedded in quartz. As the wearer's body heat changes, so does the color of the crystal. The colors are said to correspond to the wearer's mood. Mood rings are still easily found. Can a mood ring really indicate your moods just as a chameleon's colorful skin does? Find out with this challenge.

What You Need

✳ Mood ring or necklace (see the Rainforest Resources section for sources)

✳ Notebook

✳ Pencil

What You Do

1. Check out your own moods and colors by wearing a mood ring for a few days. Record the colors of your ring and your mood with each color change. Does the color of the ring accurately reflect your mood? Check the color chart below to check its accuracy.

2. At the end of a few days, look at your notebook. What color appeared the most? What color would you be most of the time if you were a chameleon?

COLOR CHART

Color	Meaning
Dark Blue	Very happy, loveable
Blue	Relaxed
Blue-Green	Somewhat relaxed
Green	Average
Amber	Feeling a little stressed
Gray	Nervous
Black	Very upset, overworked, tense

Madagascar Lemurs

Today there are 30 different species of lemurs that live only in Madagascar. Before humans came to the island there were 14 more species of lemurs. These have already become extinct because of hunting and rainforest destruction. Lemurs range in size from the tiny ground mouse lemur, which weighs only about two ounces (57 g), to the indri, which can weigh as much as 21 pounds (9.5 kg). They live primarily in the rainforest canopy and eat flowers and nectar.

The name *lemur* comes from the Latin word *lemures*, meaning ghosts. If the Madagascar rainforests continue to be destroyed at the current rate, the lemurs there may indeed become only ghosts.

The Journey Continues

It is time to journey on to the rainforests of the Americas. We are going to sail across the sea to the west and land on the shore of South America. Follow the journey on a world map. We'll be leaving from Madagascar. Are you packed up and ready to leave Africa? I hope so, because the wind is right and we're ready to sail. Climb aboard!

Crowned lemur

SOUTH AMERICAN JUNGLES 6

Imagine that our ship has landed in Aracaju, on the coast of Brazil. There we find forests of mangroves (trees with roots that grow like stilts above water), but we must press on in our journey to find the Amazon. We continue heading northwest and finally reach the Amazon River. When you imagine a rainforest, you probably think of the Amazon jungles, where butterflies, birds, and orchids bring their brilliant color to the lush greenery and mysterious Amazon River. A boat will take us part of the way into the rainforest, and then we must explore the forest on foot to get a closer look. There is much to discover in the Amazon rainforest region, but to fully explore all of the South American rainforests we must continue to travel beyond the Amazon to the Pacific Coast and the rainforests of Ecuador, Peru, and Bolivia. Did you pack enough provisions for such a journey? It will take some time, so let's get started.

Rainforest Reflection

Christopher Columbus was the first European to see the rainforests of this region. In 1498 he wrote,

Its lands are high and there are many sierras and very lofty mountains, beyond comparison with the island of Tenerife. All are most beautiful, of a thousand shapes, and all are accessible and filled with trees of a thousand kinds and tall, and they seem to touch the sky. And I am told they never lose their foliage, as I can understand, for I saw them as green and as lovely as they are in Spain in May and some of them were flowering, some bearing fruit and some in another stage, according to their nature.

The words he used to describe the rainforest are just as accurate today as they were when he first saw them centuries ago. Think about the words you would use to describe rainforests to someone who has no knowledge of them.

Happy Birthday, Baby Tamarin!

In 2001, environmentalists celebrated the birth of the 1,000th golden lion tamarin monkey in the wild. This may not seem like a big deal to you—after all, there must be tons of monkeys in South America. Well, in fact it was a very big deal. According to biologists, the population and habitat of tamarins declined so much during the 1950s and 1960s due to the development of resorts, urban sprawl, and the growth of agricultural areas that only about 200 tamarins were left in isolated areas of Rio de Janeiro and neighboring areas. The tamarin has since become a symbol of Brazil's endangered wildlife. The tamarin's cute little face, framed in a mane of orange fur like that of its lion namesake, has been printed on everything from postage stamps to souvenir T-shirts.

Efforts to save the monkey have been very productive. Now the conservationists face other hurdles—they must try to keep the population diverse and figure out where to put the growing population. Conservationists would much rather deal with these problems than face the extinction of the species.

The Company They Keep

The golden lion tamarin is not the only primate that lives in the South American rainforest. In the Atlantic forest region of South America there are 21 species and subspecies of monkeys that live along with the golden lion tamarin, including the red howler monkey, the common marmoset, the pale-fronted capuchin, the dusky titti, and the woolly spider monkey. At least 13 of the 21 species are considered endangered. The muriqui is the largest primate in South America and one of the most rare. As forests are cut, the muriqui is usually the first primate to disappear from the area. Perhaps the most endangered primate is the southern bearded saki. It lives in the rainforests of northeastern Brazil, unfortunately a very populated area of the Brazilian Amazon region. It is hunted for its meat and its tail, which is sold to tourists as a souvenir.

Cotton-Top

The cotton-top tamarin is a cousin of the golden lion tamarin. It lives in the rainforest of Colombia. By its name you can probably tell that it has a white puff of hair on the top of its head. This little tamarin is often called *blanco* in Spanish, meaning white. These tamarins really must like their hairdo, because they spend a lot of time grooming each other and making sure they look just right!

The Slow Climbing Sloth

Primates are not the only animals climbing their way through the canopy. Like monkeys, the sloth is an efficient, be it slow, tree climber. But unlike monkeys, the sloth has little or no tail to help grasp the branches. Instead, sloths use long hook-like claws to cling to

branches in the canopy. There are several different species of sloth in Central America and the jungles of the Amazon.

Sloths are *nocturnal*, meaning that they are mainly active at night. When they do sleep it is often upside down, suspended from a branch. They can grip a branch so tightly that they will not fall while they sleep. They have even been found dead, still hanging from a branch.

Sloths move very slowly. It can take a sloth an hour to move about 13 feet (4 m), and more than a day just to move to another tree. They spend most of their life in the trees, only coming to the ground once a week to go to the bathroom. The dampness of the forest and the slowness of the sloth contribute to the sloth's algae-covered fur coat. The algae color helps to *camouflage*, or hide, the sloth in the tree.

Rainforest Reflection

A sloth moves so slowly that it is often the home to hundreds of other critters. More than 900 beetles have been found living in the fur of a single sloth. Does that make your skin crawl?

How Slow Is a Sloth?

How slow is a sloth? Here's a way to find out—if you have the time.

What You Need
- Tape measure
- Masking tape
- Watch

What You Do

1. Use the tape measure to measure out a line that is 6½ feet (1.98 m) long on the floor. Mark your line with the masking tape.

2. Position yourself at one end of the line and look at your watch. Time how long it takes you to move the length of the line on all fours.

3. Now slow it down and imagine you are a sloth. See if you can take a half hour to move the length of the line. How slowly do you have to move?

Butterflies in Flight

The rainforests of South America are a butterfly's paradise. In the rainforests of central Rondônia, Brazil, there are more than 1,000 butterfly species. About 30 years ago you could expect to see at least 300 species of butterflies if you took a walk in the rainforests there, and on a good day that number might rise to 425. There are far fewer today. New species of butterflies are still being discovered in South America. In fact, 60 new species were discovered in 2001 by Smithsonian Institution scientist Jason Hall and University of Florida scientist Keith Willmott in the rainforests of Ecuador, and still more are discovered annually. It is estimated that there are 3,500 different kinds of butterflies living in Ecuador. To find out more about the butterflies in Brazil, check out the Web sites listed in the Rainforest Resources section.

Rainforest Reflection

Have you ever seen a *puddle club*? A puddle club is a group of butterflies, usually males, that gather around the edges of puddles to suck the salt and minerals out of the water.

Amazon morpho

Rusty-Tipped Page

Plant a Butterfly Garden

It is important to protect the butterflies where you live as well as those in the rainforest. Butterflies contribute to the health of our environment by serving as plant pollinators and as food for other animals (birds, mammals, spiders, and other insects). They are also very sensitive to changes in the environment, and help warn us about unhealthy changes that are taking place. A butterfly garden is a great way to attract butterflies to your home. Not only will you enjoy spotting different butterflies in your garden, but you'll also be able to watch their metamorphosis from caterpillar to adult butterfly.

What You Need

- Garden area that gets plenty of sun
- Shrubs nearby for shelter from the wind
- Host plants for caterpillars (see list, page 62)
- Nectar plants (see list, page 62)
- A grown-up to assist

What You Do

1. Pick out a sunny spot for your butterfly garden. Your garden can be in containers on a patio or in an area of your yard.

2. Provide the basics for your garden. You must have good soil, water, and some hiding places nearby (shrubs nearby).

Butterfly Spotted by Pilot

The huge, hand-sized morpho butterfly flies through the canopy and emergent layers of the rainforest with blue iridescent wings that catch the sunlight. Their wings are so brilliant that pilots flying over the rainforest have spied them from the air when the sun hits their wings.

3. To have a successful butterfly garden, plant host plants that will provide food for young caterpillars and nectar plants that will supply food for adult butterflies. Look at the lists on the next page and pick out plants from both lists. Depending on how much room you have, you may choose only three plants in your garden or you may have room for a larger assortment. Ask a grown-up to help select the plants you will plant.

4. Mist your plants early in the morning so that your butterflies will have some water to drink. Never use

pesticides in your garden. If you do, you will end up killing your butterflies. See how many different butterfly species visit your garden.

HOST PLANTS

Butterfly Weed	Milkweed
Hollyhock	False Indigo
Aster	Snapdragon
Yarrow	Fennel
Lupine	Sunflower
Burdock	

NECTAR PLANTS

Butterfly Weed	Marigold
Hollyhock	Nasturtium
Yarrow	Petunia
Gayfeather	Coneflower
Butterfly Bush	Honeysuckle
Lilac	Iris
Columbine	Coreopsis
Goldenrod	Lupine

Passionflowers Fight Back!

Not all plants are happy to have caterpillars crawling on them and eating them. The passionflower has developed many different means of attack to keep itself free from such munchers. Passionflower vines sometimes grow leaves that look like the leaves of other plants that caterpillars don't like. In this way, they disguise themselves to damaging caterpillars. Passionflowers sometimes grow things that look like butterfly eggs. When a

butterfly flies by to lay her eggs, she sees the fake eggs and thinks that the vine has already been taken by another butterfly. Some passionflower vines grow hooked hairs on their leaves that will actually kill caterpillars. When they can't do it all themselves, passionflower vines enlist ants to help them. Their flowers produce nectar for the ants and, in turn, the ants protect their host by killing the caterpillars on the plants.

Cacao tree with pods

Food of the Gods

Did you know that if it weren't for rainforests we would not have one of the most popular candies? It's true. Chocolate comes from the cacao tree, which grows in the understory of the rainforest. The cacao grew wild in South American jungles about 2,000 years before the Europeans arrived. It is believed that the Aztec ruler Montezuma entertained the explorer Cortez with a drink called *chocolatl*. It was sort of like hot cocoa with added spices and vanilla.

Does chocolate grow on trees? Well, sort of. The cacao trees have small white flowers that are pollinated by flies called *midges*. Pods form on the tree and change color, from green to yellow to a reddish-purple, as they ripen. The pods grow all over the tree, even from the trunk. The pods are pretty big, about the size of footballs.

Inside the pod is a white pulp that contains almond-sized seeds. There are about 20 to 40 seeds, or *cacao beans*, in each pod. These seeds are the start of our chocolate. The seeds need to be fermented, dried, roasted, shelled, and finally crushed into a paste. Chocolate is made from that paste. Most chocolate today comes from trees that are grown on plantations or farms, but its roots are in the rainforest! Look in the Rainforest Resources section for the Hershey Web site where you can take a virtual tour of how chocolate is made.

Make Mexican Hot Chocolate

Try this recipe for Mexican hot chocolate. It is the modern version of the early drink that the Mayans and the Aztecs drank. It is said that Montezuma drank many cups of chocolate every day. Some of them were even mixed with cornmeal, a spice called achiote, and other spices. You'll find this version is a bit spicier than the hot chocolate you usually drink.

What You Need

- A grown-up to assist
- 3 cups (710 ml) scalded milk (heated to just below the boiling point)
- Saucepan
- Grater
- 2 squares good-quality dark chocolate
- Whisk
- 2 tablespoons (25 g) sugar
- 1 tablespoon (17 g) cinnamon
- 1 cup (237 ml) boiling water
- Pinch salt

What You Do

1. Ask a grown-up to help with the cooking.
2. Pour the milk into the saucepan and heat it until just before it boils. It will get a bit foamy.
3. Grate the chocolate over the saucepan and stir with the whisk to help the chocolate melt.
4. Add the sugar, cinnamon, and water. Boil for two minutes.
5. Add the salt.
6. Stir the mixture and pour it into mugs or, if you'd like to drink it like the Mayans did, pour it into small bowls.

What Else Comes from the Rainforest?

Many other items and foods originate in rainforests. Did you know that chewing gum has its roots in the rainforest? At one time the base for all chewing gum was the white resin, called *chicle*, of the *chicozapote*, or sapodilla, tree found in the rainforests of Guatemala and Honduras. The tree is tapped, similar to how maple trees are tapped for sap. The fluid flows from a slash in the bark and is collected to make gum. After the chicle sap is tapped, the sap is boiled, cooled, and formed into *marquetas*, or blocks, that are shipped to the gum factory. Chewing gum is now primarily made from synthetic or man-made bases instead of chicle, but if you'd like a taste of chewing gum still made from chicle, check out the Rainforest Resources section for some sources. You might even find a kit to make your own chewing gum.

Rainforest Expedition

There are even more products and plants in our homes that originate in the rainforests of South America and elsewhere. Take an expedition through your home to see how many of these items you can find.

- **Allspice** (look in the spice cabinet): Guatemala, southeastern Mexico, Honduras
- **Vanilla**: Southeastern Mexico, Central America, West Indies, northern South America, Madagascar
- **Ramie** (check your clothing labels): Brazil and the Philippines
- **Rubber**: South America
- **Philodendron**: South America
- **Zebra plant**: Brazil
- **Brazil nuts**: Brazil and the Amazon
- **Pineapple**: Hawaii and the Ivory Coast of Africa
- **Coffee**: Costa Rica
- **Banana**: Costa Rica and others
- **Crude oil**: The Amazon, Papua New Guinea, Burma, Nigeria, and others
- **Gold**: Ghana, Papua New Guinea, and others
- **Lumber**: every rainforest

The People of the Rainforest

Many different tribes live in the rainforests of South America. The Jivaro (pronounced HEE-va-ro) people of Ecuador all speak the same language. Many tribes belong to this group, including the Shuar, Huambisa, Aguaruna, Achuar, Huaorani, and Shiviar people.

These tribes do not roam the rainforest looking for food like many other rainforest people. Jivaro men usually don't travel more than a day's walk to find game to hunt for their tribe. They hunt with blowguns that fire darts poisoned with curare. *Curare* is a poison that is made from a variety of rainforest plants. The Jivaro also use rifles on occasion. Besides hunting game, Jivaro men fish in the streams and rivers. They also eat fruits and insects from the rainforest. The women of the tribe cook, take care of the children and animals, and cultivate the land. It is common for families to grow yams, corn, bananas, sugar cane, squash, cotton, and peanuts on their land in the rainforest.

Once one of the fiercest groups of warriors, the Jivaro practiced the ancient ritual of headhunting. They became well known for their ability to shrink heads. To shrink a head, the skin was first removed from the skull. Hot sand and stones were placed inside the skin of the head and the burnt flesh was then scraped out. This was done until the head was completely hard and dried. The entire head was then blackened with charcoal and the lips were pinned shut. One Jivaro belief is that each tribe has a limited number of souls. For a new baby to be born, a tribe member must die. They believe that shrinking an enemy's head is a way to steal an enemy's soul and add it to the tribe's supply. Although methods differ among tribes, in all cases the practice of head shrinking is based on their spirituality. The Jivaro no longer practice head hunting but ceremonial head shrinking still exists.

The Tribe Today

For centuries, rainforest tribes have hunted for their food, fished in clean rivers, picked fruit from the trees, and cured their illnesses with medicines they made from the plants of the rainforest. Their way of life is changing. The rainforest can't support the Shuar and many other tribes anymore. The destruction of the rainforest by loggers, oil drillers, and farmers has taken its toll on many tribes. They need money for supplies, education, and emergency transportation. A group of Shuar are now organized to make and sell their crafts. For many years they made necklaces and other crafts from the seeds, feathers, insects, and bones they obtained while they hunted for their own use. Now they make these to sell. The money that they earn helps them retain their way of life in the rainforest. Look in the Rainforest Resources section for more information on Shuar crafts.

The Roosevelts, Jungle Explorers

Theodore Roosevelt was the 26th president of the United States. After his presidency he led an expedition into the jungles of South America, which had never been mapped. His explorations added 900 miles of the Amazon to the map. Accompanying him were Frank Chapman, curator of ornithology (birds) for the American Museum of Natural History; his friend, Father Zahm; his son Kermit; two scientists that Chapman recommended; and quite a few journalists. The expedition was planned to concentrate on the birds and mammals of the jungle. The explorers traveled deep into the uncharted Amazon wilderness and saw things that only the Amazon natives had seen before.

Teddy Roosevelt's expedition was an amazing trip for that time and took a great deal of courage. They traveled with canoes, provisions for only 40 days, and little else. When they needed more canoes they made dugout canoes from trees they cut down on the trip. He wrote about his trip in the book *Through the Brazilian Wilderness*. It is still considered one of the great masterpieces among explorers' records.

In 1992, Tweed Roosevelt, Teddy's great-grandson, re-created the famous trip undertaken in 1913. He had a much easier time, traveling with lightweight boats, insect repellent, modern medicine, nourishing food, accurate maps, communication equipment, and water filtration systems. He found that much of the jungle remained as it had been 78 years before, and yet he saw that civilization had crept in as well. When Teddy Roosevelt visited the region, many of the natives had never seen anyone who lived outside their forest. Now some of them wear clothes made elsewhere and even hunt with guns.

Onward

It is hard to leave the South American rainforest. There is still so much to discover, but this leg of our trip is over. The Rainforest Resources section lists other books, movies, and Web sites to help satisfy your curiosity about the Amazon and other rainforests in South America. Now check your passport and get ready for more adventure.

SOUTH ASIAN AND MALAYSIAN RAINFORESTS

7

For the next leg of our journey we must hop a plane and fly across the Pacific Ocean. For a long time we will see nothing but water below us. Finally we'll see some islands that look like dots in the open sea. Among the many dots we see in the water is the tiny island we will be landing on. Our first stop is the island of Borneo, and after our visit there we will continue to many other rainforests in this region. We will visit the rainforests of Indonesia, Thailand, Burma, India, Papua New Guinea, and even Australia. Look at a map to see where we're headed. I hope you packed well. We will be traveling on foot a great deal. So grab your bags and let's head into the rainforests of Borneo.

Pack for Borneo Game

Imagine we've found some local guides to take us into the forests of Borneo. To get to our rainforest destination we first need to board a small boat and travel up the river. Then we must hike into the rainforest on foot. It will take us about a month just to get to the deep forest, because we will be mostly on foot and the terrain is difficult. We must pack only what we can carry. What will you bring? Play this game to help you pack your backpack for our extended rainforest trip.

What You Need
✳ A group of friends

What You Do
1. Sit in a circle with your friends. Think carefully about the items you will need to bring for a one-month journey into the rainforest.

2. To start the game the first player says, "I'm going to Borneo and I'm bringing _____." The player must then name an item to pack in his or her backpack for the trip. The item has to be able to fit in a backpack. The second player repeats the phrase, "I'm going to Borneo and I'm bringing _____." This player repeats what the first player said and then adds a new item. The third player continues the game by repeating the items players one and two said and adding a third, and so on. The game continues until someone forgets an item or the group feels that the backpack is full.

3. Continue this game with the Rainforest Challenge found at the end of the book.

Sneakers, Hiking Boots, or Sandals?

What would you wear on your feet for a trek into the jungle? Would you wear sneakers, hiking boots, sandals, or go barefoot? Barefoot? You probably would never think of going barefoot into the jungle, but the natives do. If you wore hiking boots in the jungle your feet would probably become covered with leeches. After trampling through the wet, muddy forest floor where the leeches live, your hiking boots would get damp and would not dry. Since leeches love dampness, the leeches will love your hiking boots! It's something to think about.

Paradise or Not?

To many people the word *rainforest* is synonymous with paradise, but is it really paradise? Ask the teams that raced through the Borneo rainforest during Eco-Challenge 2000. Eco-Challenge is an expedition race. Teams of men and women race nonstop for 6 to 12 days, rafting, mountain biking, horseback riding, mountaineering, and kayaking across 200 miles of rugged territory using only maps and compasses for orientation. They are faced with many challenges from the environment. The teams that raced through the Borneo rainforest in 2000 faced falling trees, storms, leeches, low visibility, mud, and still more leeches. One challenger even had to receive medical attention for a leech in her eye. But like any other competition, the challenge of winning is worth it all.

The Penan

Whether or not you call the rainforest paradise, it's home to many people. The Penan are a tribe of nomadic hunter-gatherers who live deep in the Borneo rainforest. The headhunting practices of other tribes drove them deep into the rainforest many years ago. They are a peaceful people with no history of murder.

The Penan language does not even have a word that means *thief*. They live in groups of three to four families who share everything. All food and property is shared among the families. Their survival depends on this principle. Selfishness is something that could cause great harm to them. Imagine you live among the Penan and the hunters have gone out to hunt. One of the hunters is very successful, but perhaps the others are not. When the hunters return, all of the hunt is shared among the families. Perhaps the next time the hunters go out, one of the other hunters is successful and again they share the hunt among the families.

The Penan believe the creator gave them the rainforest. They believe that the animals and plants are for their use, and that they all have souls. The Penan only

use what they need. There is no waste among the families. Their belief is that they only borrow from the rainforest. That also implies that they must not waste and must give back.

The men hunt with blowpipes and poisoned darts. Penan hunters never travel more than a day away from their families when they are hunting. If you traveled for a month to reach a remote Penan family in their open-walled lean-to, which has a roof held up by poles, you would not see many things. You might look at them and think that they are very poor, but they would look back at you and think that you are very poor because you are very far from your family. They will share what food they have with you, knowing that you probably cannot survive in the rainforest without them.

The Penan, like many native people of the rainforests, are struggling to keep their rainforests from being cut down. Many have been relocated to government resettlements, and still others find "no trespassing" signs in parts of their rainforest. But the rainforest is part of the Penan and the Penan are part of the rainforest. The boundary between the people and nature is blurred when we talk about rainforests. These people have their own niche, or part, in the rainforest community and are crucial to the survival of the whole ecosystem, just like any other creature in the system. Many groups are trying to help the Penan and other rainforest people in their struggle to save their homes. You can help, too. Check out things that you can do in Chapter 10 and in the Rainforest Resources section for groups that are helping to save the rainforests and their peoples.

Communicate with Message Sticks

The Penan use message sticks to communicate with each other when they travel. They leave the sticks in the rainforest along their routes to tell other hunters where to look for game, to alert a traveler to a danger ahead, or to relay some other message. Other groups, such as the Aborigines of Australia, also use message sticks to communicate. When there was no written language, the message sticks helped the courier to remember the message he carried. Here's a way to create your own message sticks.

What You Need

- Wooden dowels or sticks at least ½ inch (1.27 cm) thick
- Pencil
- Acrylic paints
- Paintbrushes

What You Do

1. Think about the message you want to tell someone. It could be "I love you," "Have a nice day," or some other message you choose. Have you ever seen a pictogram? *Pictograms* use pictures to represent words. Think about the pictures that you could draw on your stick to represent the words of your message.

2. Draw the pictures on your stick.

3. Use the paints to fill in your drawings and decorate your stick.

4. Share your stick with friends. Can they interpret your message?

The World's Largest Flower

OK, so you've decided to continue the journey into the rainforests of Southeast Asia. You are well aware of the obstacles you face and are prepared with a backpack full of essentials. Let's visit the jungles of Thailand, Sumatra, and Malaysia. When you enter any of the rainforests in this region the jungle surrounds you and you are quickly surrounded by sound, just as in the other rainforests you have visited. You hear birds, frogs, insects, and other creatures as you make your way through the jungle, and then it hits you—an awful smell, as if an animal has died and is rotting on the forest floor. You look around and there to your left is a huge flower. It is the largest flower you have ever seen, and you realize the smell is actually coming from the flower. You walk over to get a closer look. The flower is roughly three feet (91 cm) across. It is a rafflesia, the largest flower in the world. The rafflesia is a *parasite*, meaning it feeds off another plant. In this case, the flower bud grows inside the root of the host plant. It then breaks through to the outside and becomes the large flower we see. It smells like rotting flesh because it's trying to attract flies.

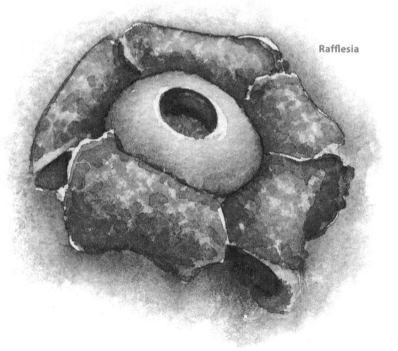

Rafflesia

The Primates of the Jungle

People are not the only primates to inhabit the South Asian rainforests. There are macaques, gibbons, tarsiers, langurs, and orangutans that also make their home in the rainforests. Many different characteristics define a primate. For instance, primates have very mobile fingers, toes, hands, and feet that have adapted for grasping. Their fingertips are sensitive to touch and are protected by nails instead of claws like other animals. They also have a bigger, more complex brain relative to their body size and their eyes are in the front of the face.

The First Monkey, a Tale of the Philippines

Here's a *pourquoi* (which means "why" in French) tale from the Philippines. Like other *pourquoi* tales of long ago, it tries to explain why something is the way it is. In this case, it sets out to explain the origin of the monkeys that live in the island rainforests. After you read it, see if you can come up with your own tale to explain the origin of monkeys.

In ancient times, the goddess of weaving lived deep in the forest with her apprentice. She taught the young girl how to gather cotton, spin it, weave it into cloth, and sew it into beautiful clothing. The apprentice learned everything well, but she was lazy and always looked for the easier way out.

One day the goddess asked her to make a dress. She gave her all the instructions again for gathering the cotton, spinning it, weaving it, and sewing it, but the apprentice was eager to finish the dress and decided to use a piece of leather instead. She draped the leather around herself and stood before the goddess. When the goddess saw that her apprentice did not follow her directions she became very angry and she decided to punish the girl. She waved her stick at the girl and the leather formed around her body. When the girl looked in the mirror she saw that the stick had become a tail and the leather now covered her body like fur. The apprentice had been turned into a monkey!

Thailand's Monkey Business

Farmers in Thailand have figured out a way to harvest more coconuts. They have trained macaques to climb the trees for them. The monkeys are taken from their mothers and placed in schools that are like dog training schools. They learn how to select a ripe coconut and twist it right off of the tree for the farmer waiting below. The monkeys can pick 800 to 1,000 coconuts in six to eight hours of work after being trained for three to six months. Many feel that the monkey population would be endangered if this program didn't exist, since many of the forests have been cut down. What

do you think? Does putting them to work help or hurt the monkeys?

There Is No G at the End of Orangutan!

The orangutan is the primate with the most frequently mispronounced name. It is native to the forests of Borneo and Sumatra. The name *orangutan* actually means "jungle man" in the Malay language, and at 5 feet (1.5 m) tall and about 220 pounds (100 kg), male orangs really fit the bill. Orangutans have reddish hair and live in the rainforest canopy, about 20 to 100 feet (6 to 30 m) above the forest floor. They spend most of the day searching for fruit, flowers, insects, and leaves to eat. Like gorillas, they build a nest above the ground to sleep in each night.

In the shrinking rainforest habitat, orangs have become easy prey for smugglers and poachers, who capture them for the pet trade and for meat. Some of the more fortunate ones are rescued from the smugglers and put into rehabilitation centers before being released back into the wild. It is very hard to rehabilitate many of the poached orangs because they only give birth every eight to nine years and the young remain with their mothers until they are about six years old. Like human children, orangs need to be taught all they need to know to survive.

Think Tank

If you would like to get an up-close view of an orangutan, visit the Smithsonian National Zoological Park in Washington, D.C. There you can watch the orangs commute over the O-Line to the Think Tank to engage in activities with researchers that demonstrate their language skills, social interaction, and their ability to use tools. It's one of the few places where you can actually watch researchers at work. The orangs will amaze you with their intelligence and abilities as they work with animal behaviorists on the computer, constructing simple sentences with the touch screen. Check out the Rainforest Resources section for information on visiting the zoological park.

Make a Wayang Klitik Puppet

The shadow puppets of Indonesia are very well known. The Indonesian people of Java make three different shadow puppets: *Wayang kulit*, which are shadow puppets created from leather; *Wayang golek*, which are three-dimensional puppets made with wooden rods; and Wayang klitik. *Wayang klitik* puppets are flat, wooden, painted puppets. They are usually made to perform adventures of Javanese Majapahit Empire heroes. Here's a version of the Wayang klitik puppets that you can make to tell your own rainforest tale. Choose a favorite folktale, or select a portion of *The Jungle Book* by Rudyard Kipling to perform with your puppets.

What You Need

- Pencil
- Cardboard
- Scissors
- Assorted acrylic paints
- Paintbrush
- A grown-up to assist
- Needle
- Paper clip
- Wooden dowel or pencil
- Tape

What You Do

1. Draw a rainforest animal, such as a python, a tiger, or an orangutan, on the cardboard. The animal should be at least seven inches long (18 cm).

2. Cut out your animal.

3. Use the paints to decorate your animal as the Java people do with their puppets. They often use bright colors and exaggerate features to make them more theatrical.

4. Ask a grown-up to use the needle to poke two holes, the width of the paper clip, into the center of the animal.

5. Pull the paper clip slightly apart and push one side through one hole from the back. When the first side is through, push it through the second hole. You should see only a loop on the front side of the puppet.

6. Tape the dowel to the paper clip on the back of the puppet to manipulate the puppet. Your puppet is now

ready for your show. Use your puppets with a screen and a light source so that you will see their shadows as you tell your story. The next activity will help you to create your very own theater for your performance.

Note: If you made a snake puppet, you will need to position a dowel on either end for balance, so make two sets of holes.

Construct a Jungle Book Theater

Can you think of a better theater for your puppets to perform in than a theater inspired by Rudyard Kipling's famous book, *The Jungle Book*? Here's how to make your own.

What You Need
- A grown-up to assist
- Scissors
- Large cardboard box (microwave-oven size)
- Light-green tissue paper
- Tape or stapler
- Dark-green tissue paper
- Glue stick
- Light source (flashlight, window, or lamp)

What You Do
1. Ask a grown-up to cut out the back of the box so there are now two openings.
2. Cover one opening with the light-green tissue paper to create your screen. Attach the screen to the box with the stapler or tape.
3. Cut out a few leaf shapes from the dark-green tissue paper. Spread glue on them with the glue stick. Glue them around the edges of the box opening and press them onto the light-green tissue paper so that it looks like the trees and vines are edging the theater.
4. Place your theater box on a table with the light source behind the box. The stronger the light source, the clearer your shadow puppets will look.
5. Hold your puppet between the light source and the screen. You are now ready for your show. Practice holding the puppet so that its shadow is nice and clear to the audience.

Create a simple story about the rainforest. You might want to choose a story from *The Jungle Book*, or maybe a story about an animal that you have learned about. One easy way to create a story is to be sure your story has a beginning, a problem that can be solved, and an ending that solves the problem. There are many other types of stories also. See what type works best with your characters. Also, think about other shadow puppets that you could add to your show. Have fun and put on a great show for your family and friends.

Shere Khan, Lord of the Jungle

Shere Khan may have been the villain in *The Jungle Book*, but in reality tigers have been victims throughout the rainforests of Asia. The number of surviving tigers has decreased from 100,000 to 5,000 in the past 50 years, mainly due to the destruction of the rainforests. The world's smallest living tiger, the Sumatran tiger, weighs about 275 pounds (125 kg), about half of the weight of a Siberian or Indian tiger. This "island" tiger has already disappeared from the islands of Java and Bali. There are now fewer than 500 Sumatran tigers living in the wild. Conservation efforts are underway and may be the last hope for these magnificent animals.

To Camouflage or Not to Camouflage?

Many flowers are brightly colored to attract creatures that will pollinate them. Some animals, such as poison dart frogs, use color to warn others not to bother them. Other creatures, such as brightly colored male birds, use color to attract mates. Then there are those creatures like the sloth, which use their colors to disguise themselves in the rainforest. You might think that the patterned fur of tigers and other large cats would be outstanding in the green forest, but their stripes, spots, or blotches actually look like the effect of sunlight filtering through the leaves of the forest. The patterned fur of large cats is camouflage, and it helps them remain unseen by the prey they stalk.

In this activity you get to create your own rainforest creature and decide whether or not it should be camouflaged.

What You Need

- ✺ Markers
- ✺ Paper

What You Do

1. Think about all of the different creatures that live in the rainforest, and then invent your own creature to live in an Asian rainforest. Will it be a mammal, insect, bird, or perhaps a reptile or amphibian?

2. Decide which layer of the rainforest your creature will live in. For example, will it live on the rainforest floor like the tarantula does, or up high in the canopy with the monkeys?

3. Decide whether your creature will need to camouflage itself in the forest. What existing rainforest creature will prey upon it? Decide what your creature will eat. Does it need a long tongue like a chameleon's or a beak like a bird's? Does it need claws or suction cups on its feet?

4. Draw a picture of your creature. Color your new rainforest creature as it would be seen in the forest. Last, give your creature a name.

Lucy Evelyn Cheesman, Jungle Explorer

The creatures in rainforests are definitely unique and worth studying. That's what Lucy Evelyn Cheesman (1881–1969) thought when she embarked on her exploration of Papua New Guinea. When she was young she desperately wanted to be a veterinarian, but at that time, women were not allowed to attend veterinary school. Instead, she took a job at the Zoological Society's garden in London. Her job was to be the keeper of the run-down insect house. She became fascinated with the insects she kept, and shared her excitement with others.

It wasn't until she was 42 years old that she began her days as an explorer. By that time she had established herself with the Zoological Society, and she jumped at the chance to travel for them. And once she began traveling, she didn't stop. She wrote many books about her South Pacific rainforest expeditions. She traveled lightly, with only a string hammock, insect trays, and some necessities, and she learned to rely on the natives for all her other needs. She was a middle-aged, European white woman who found herself living and traveling with native tribes that practiced cannibalism. She did not press her ideas of proper behavior on them, nor did they on her, and so they developed a mutual respect. During her many expeditions she wrote in her journals and collected specimens for English museums. Her fieldwork was interrupted by World War II, but she turned her attention to helping the Allied forces, which included her native England, by supplying them with detailed information about the islands she had explored so well.

Gone Batty

As any jungle explorer knows, many birds make their home in the Asian rainforests, but they are not the only creatures that fly about the rainforest canopy. The rainforests of Asia are the home of many species of bats. As night falls on the rainforest, the birds leave the skies and the bats begin to emerge from their roosts under bark and in trees and take flight. The bats are extremely important to the health of the rainforest. They pollinate flowers and spread seeds across the forest. Some bats eat flower nectar, just like hummingbirds and butterflies. Others eat insects, and still others eat fruit. Unlike insect-eating bats, which use sound in a process called *echolocation* to orient them when they fly, fruit bats rely on sight. The fruit bats are sometimes called flying foxes, although they're not foxes at all. The world's largest bat, a fruit bat called the *kalang*,

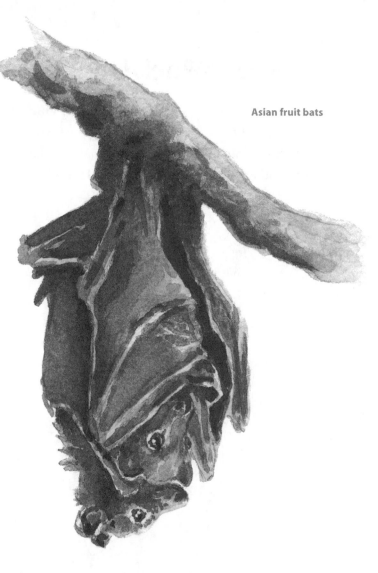

Asian fruit bats

has a wingspan greater than 5 feet (1.5 m) and lives in the South Asian forests. How tall are you? Can you imagine a bat with a wingspan that stretches out longer than you are? Now that's a big bat!

Time to Pack Up

Well, the time has come to move on. Our next two stops will bring us a bit closer to home. We are going to hop a plane for our first destination, Hawaii. Like the other islands we have visited, Hawaii lies south of the Tropic of Cancer and north of the Tropic of Capricorn. Can you find the Hawaiian islands on a map? After we visit there for a while we'll hop back on the plane and fly east to the Caribbean to visit some other islands that are dotted with rainforests. So grab your packs and get ready to board.

ISLAND RAINFORESTS OF THE PACIFIC AND CARIBBEAN

8

As soon as we touch down on the Hawaiian island of Oahu we're greeted with sweet-smelling flowers, such as oleander and orchids, that are placed in a ring over our heads. This garland or wreath is called a *lei* in Hawaiian. The flowers fall around your shoulders, and their aroma pulls you into the island. All this is great, but hey, we're still in the city. Where are the forests? Actually, it will take some time to reach the forests. You see, there aren't many left, due to the widespread development of the islands. So get ready for a short flight to another of the Hawaiian islands.

String an Aloha Maui Lei

Just a short flight from Oahu is the island of Maui, known as the Valley Isle. Our plane sets down and we are greeted warmly with another beautiful lei of flowers placed around our necks. Of course, it would be wonderful if we could take them home, but that's impossible. We have too many stops ahead of us for them to survive. So instead, here's a way to make your very own flower lei. Keep in mind that May 1, commonly known as May Day, is known as Lei Day in Hawaii and is a great time to celebrate and make your own lei.

What You Need

- Fresh flowers (azaleas, lilies, and carnations are some good choices)
- Needle
- String or unwaxed dental floss

What You Do

1. Make sure the flowers are fresh and not wilted, then remove each blossom from its stem by carefully plucking it from the base.

2. Begin by threading the needle with a length of string or floss measured to the length of your finished lei.

3. String the flowers all in the same direction, just as you would string popcorn. Place the needle up through the center of the flower at the base and pull the needle and string through the flower to the front of the blossom. Add the next flower by guiding the needle up through its base and into the center and so on.

4. When you have completed stringing the flowers, join the two ends together and knot them.

Note: There are many lei craft activities that use straws or paper flowers. They are also fun to try, especially if you are unable to string real flowers.

Finding the Forest

There was a time when Maui's rainforest was easy to find, but much of the forest has disappeared due to development and farming. Now in order to visit Maui's rainforest we must head into the higher elevations of the island to Waikamoi, about 6,000 feet (1,829 m) above sea level. Waikamoi, a nature conservancy preserve, is the most easily reached rainforest left on Maui. There are other rainforests, but they are much too remote for most people. The first thing you would probably notice at Waikamoi is the spongy earth beneath your feet. The ground is covered in soft *humus*, similar to peat moss, and other decaying matter that makes it spongy. It is extremely important to walk very softly and carefully on this ground. When the ground is broken it becomes easy for seeds and spores of nonnative or alien plant species to grow. Plants that are not native to Hawaii can take over the forest and endanger the native rainforest plants.

Aliens Are Not from Outer Space

It is astonishing that more than 70 percent of the species that have become extinct in the United States

Rainforest Reflection

The early Polynesians of Hawaii created leis for sacred rituals, as ornaments for dancers, and as symbols of rank in the community. Early leis were created with shells, seeds, and other materials. Flowers began to appear in leis in the 19th century, when more traders and travelers came to the islands and made the flower leis more popular. Native flowers, such as orchids and plumeria, as well as nonnative carnations and roses, which were brought by travelers, were strung into beautiful leis to celebrate special occasions and to honor the recipient, just as you give your mom a flower corsage on Mother's Day to honor her. Although there are now many versions of the traditional leis, the flower leis have become a symbol of a Hawaiian welcome or a reflection of the aloha spirit.

are from Hawaii, which makes up only 0.2 percent of the country's land base. In addition, almost 30 percent of the species currently listed on the endangered species list are found only in Hawaii. Why is this so? Well, one reason is the introduction of alien species to the islands. No, these aliens are not from outer space. They are plants and animals that are brought to the islands from other places. These alien species compete with the native species in Hawaii, or they develop a niche that is damaging to native species. Most of these alien species do not have any natural predators in

Hawaii, so their population keeps growing. For example, in the late 1700s pigs were brought to Hawaii for food. The pigs were too plentiful to control, and soon they were all over the place. They dug up roots of

Pigs are an alien species to the Hawaiian rainforests.

native plants, ate others, and created large puddles that became the breeding ground for mosquitoes that carried diseases to native birds and threatened their populations. Introducing an alien species into the Hawaiian rainforest is like pulling a card out of a tall house of cards. If a nonnative species, like the pig, causes a negative impact on native species, like the birds, the whole ecosystem can collapse. In the next activity you'll see how two alien species, the mongoose and the rat, turned the Hawaiian ecosystem upside down. But first, the following sections will describe some of the unique native populations of Hawaii that are sometimes threatened by alien species.

Meeting the Natives

Would you believe that Hawaii has only two native mammals, the hoary bat and the monk seal? A *mammal* is a warm-blooded animal with hair that feeds its young with milk. However, what the islands lack in mammal species they certainly make up for in bird species. There are 78 species of birds that are native to Hawaii, although 26 are now extinct and 30 are presently on the endangered species list. In fact, eight of these endangered birds call the rainforest of Waikamoi home. One is the crested honeycreeper,

Rainforest Reflection

Many people have written about our wild environments. John Muir was a naturalist who spent much of his life in the forests writing about his observations. He recorded many things, including this entry from his 1911 book *My First Summer in the Sierra*: "When we try to pick out anything by itself, we find it hitched to everything else in the Universe." Think about what he wrote. Can you put this in your own words?

known in Hawaiian as Akohekohe, which is found only in the Waikamoi rainforest and nowhere else in the world. It was once believed to be extinct, but the discovery of a couple of active nests gave conservationists some hope for the species. Other birds that inhabit the forests of Hawaii include the Apapane, 'I'iwi, Maui parrotbill, and Akiapola'au. Many of Hawaii's birds are small, brightly colored descendants of Hawaiian honeycreepers. It is believed that at least 23 species and 24 subspecies of the Hawaiian honeycreeper evolved on the islands.

Crested honeycreeper

'I'iwi

Isolation Breeds Uniqueness

The Hawaiian Islands, like the Galápagos Islands, are isolated from other lands. The same holds true for Australia and Madagascar. These remote places have many creatures that are not found in other places in the world. Can you guess why? Well, the ancestors of Hawaii's native creatures came across the ocean, probably by chance, from very distant lands. That means that they either swam or flew to the islands from other lands. That is how many creatures come to live on any island. Once on the island, the creatures did not have to compete with the predators and diseases from their homeland. The species then evolved into the creatures that are found there today. Some of the birds in Hawaii have developed long curved bills that are adapted to drinking nectar from flowers. Others developed changes in their color and size to suit the Hawaiian forests. This also explains why Hawaii does not have any native reptiles or amphibians. How would they have arrived in the islands? They can't fly like the birds, and it is difficult for reptiles and amphibians to swim very long distances.

Play the Mongoose on the Loose Game

The mongoose was brought to Hawaii in 1883 by the Hilo Planters Association to control nonnative, or alien, rats that had come over on boats and were causing damage to sugarcane fields. The plan was not successful. Hawaiians soon learned that rats are nocturnal, meaning they come out at night, while the mongoose hunts for food in the daytime. Even so, the mongooses did get many of the rats in the sugarcane fields, but they also hunted other animals on the islands. They became serious predators to ground-nesting birds, such as the nene goose, and many seabirds. So the plan pretty much backfired.

See firsthand how the mongoose caused such damage while playing Mongoose on the Loose.

What You Need

- 9 friends
- Open area to play, either inside or outside
- 4 chairs or trees to hide behind
- Timer

What You Do

1. Pick one player to be the mongoose, four players to be the rats, and four players to be the nene goose eggs.

2. If you're playing inside, position the chairs around the open area. Each nene goose egg should claim a tree or chair to hide behind.

3. Set the timer for 30 seconds. When someone says "Go," the rats should run around all over the playing area. The mongoose has 30 seconds to tag a rat or a nene goose egg. When the timer buzzer rings the mongoose must bring his tagged "food" back to the starting place.

4. The tagged "foods" must remain out of play until the mongoose has tagged three foods. Once three are tagged, the first tagged food then becomes a mongoose. Continue playing the game in 30-second intervals until all of the nene goose eggs are tagged.

5. Which were easier to tag? The mongooses that are loose in Hawaii probably find that the nene goose eggs are an easy meal, just as they are in this game. Think about the future of the nene goose population in Hawaii. What do you think can be done to help the geese?

Kauai, the Garden Isle

Just a short flight from Maui is the island of Kauai. The best way to visit this stop on our Hawaiian tour is by helicopter. We're headed to Mt. Waialeale (prounced wy-ah-lay-AH-lay), a collapsed volcano. While some Hawaiian rainforests receive more than 250 inches (635 cm) of rain per year, Mt. Waialeale can receive more than twice that, which makes it the wettest spot in the world. It rains so much because the tropical trade winds cool as they flow up and over Mt. Waialeale's steep slopes, then condense at the top of the mountain to form a cloud. All that moisture makes for a lot of rain. It is an amazing sight to see the col-

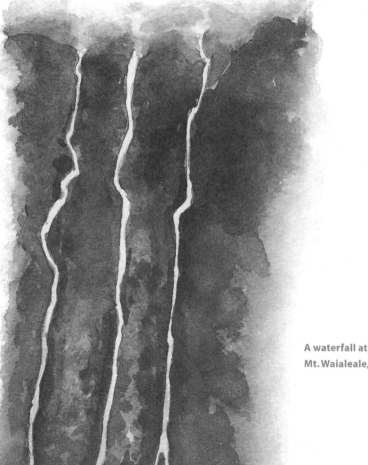

A waterfall at
Mt. Waialeale, Hawaii

lapsed volcano covered in green ferns and dripping with hundreds of waterfalls that pour down the sides of the crater.

Catching the Next Flight

It's time to head back to the Honolulu airport on the island of Oahu and catch our flight to the islands in the Caribbean. The Hawaiian rainforests we are leaving in Hawaii need some serious help if they are to survive. See Chapter 10 for things you can do to help the rainforests in Hawaii.

Let's check out the condition of the rainforests in the Caribbean. Our first stop is the island of Puerto Rico. Puerto Rico is one of the islands that stretch in an arc from Florida, in the United States, to the country of Venezuela. They were formed by volcanoes and are called volcanic islands. On some islands the volcanoes are still active. As on other islands, there are species of plants and animals here that are not found anywhere else in the world. The small island of Jamaica boasts 4 mammal, 26 bird, 20 amphibian, 27 reptile, and more than 900 plant species that are not found anywhere else. As we begin our descent we see the islands of Cuba, Jamaica, Haiti, and the Dominican Republic. The next island in the chain is Puerto Rico, followed by the Virgin Islands and many others. The wheels of our plane are down, and we are ready for our next adventure.

El Yunque

Our first stop is the Caribbean National Forest, only about 25 miles (40 km) outside of the city of San Juan, Puerto Rico. The forest, known locally as El Yunque, is found in the Sierra de Luquilo Mountains. At over 28,000 acres (11,331 ha) of land, it is the largest parcel of public land in Puerto Rico. It is also the only tropical rainforest in the United States' national forest system. El Yunque is named after the good spirit Yuquiyu. The ancient Taino Indians, who lived in the islands, believed that Yuquiyu ruled the rainforest and protected them. Like all other rainforests, El Yunque is alive with sound. Each rainforest, however, has its own unique sounds from the creatures that inhabit it. El Yunque is filled with the sounds of native chattering birds, among them the squawk of the Puerto Rican parrot. At night and when it rains, the forest becomes alive with the co-kee call of the tiny tree frogs, called *coquis*, that are famous on the island.

Write a Coqui Sound Poem

Coqui tree frog

It's hard to believe that the loudest and noisiest sound in the Puerto Rican rainforest comes out of a tiny tree frog that is only about one inch (2.5 cm) long. These little frogs are so noisy that the male coqui frog call can reach 100 decibels only a meter (3.3 feet) away. You can compare this to the sound of an orchestra in an auditorium, which generally ranges between 40 and 100 decibels. There are 13 species of tree frogs in the rainforest, but the famous co-kee call is produced by only two—the forest coqui and the common coqui. The other 11 species each have their own call. Coquis are so highly regarded in Puerto Rico that the tiny tree frog is a national symbol. Many stories, songs, and poems have been written about them. Write your own words of praise for the little coquis in a sound poem about their famous call.

What You Need

🜚 Paper

🜚 Pencil

What You Do

1. A sound poem uses words to describe the sound of the subject. For example, if you were to write a sound poem about rain, you might use the words *drip, drop* to describe the sound of the rain falling outside. Look at the Web sites in the Rainforest Resources section for some examples of sound poems before you begin writing.

2. Focus your poem on the co-kee sound the coqui makes. What other words could you use to describe the little frog's call? Make a list of them to include in your poem.

3. Using the words you came up with, write your poem. Poems have a rhythm, like a song. Your poem does not have to rhyme, although it could, but it should have some type of rhythm or beat. Play around with the words to develop the rhythm of your poem.

4. When you finish writing your poem, try writing another poem about a sound you hear every day. Was the second poem easier to write than the poem about the tree frog?

State of the Forests

We are happy to find that Puerto Rico's rainforest has grown back naturally, after Europeans cleared much of it for lumber before 1900. In 1903 only 0.4 percent of the land was still forested, but by 1978, after the collapse of the sugarcane industry, the forest covered 32 percent of the island. Protection is now underway for much of the island's natural rainforest.

More Islands, Hurricanes, and the Rainforests

Many more islands in the Caribbean are dotted with rainforests. Among them is Dominica. It sits between the islands of Guadeloupe and Martinique. Dominica is the most mountainous and the most forested of the Lesser Antilles islands. Rainforest destruction is caused by forest clearing for plantations and farming, but also by hurricanes that rip apart many of the rainforest trees. When Hurricane David blew through the islands in 1979, Dominica lost roughly five million trees to hurricane damage. Many of the trees were uprooted. Branches were torn and the fruiting and flowering cycles were disrupted. It could take 50 or more years for the rainforests to fully recover. These natural disasters are impossible to prevent, but the organized clearing for farming and development by islanders is more preventable. Organizations are working hard to conserve the remaining forests on these islands.

Flight Out of the Tropics

Well, it's time to get back to the mainland to visit North America's temperate rainforests. Our flight will head northwest to an area rich in old-growth trees and many creatures not found in the tropical rainforests. It's a bit cooler in the next rainforest, so a change in wardrobe is definitely in order. So pack up and let's go.

TEMPERATE RAINFORESTS 9 OF THE PACIFIC NORTHWEST

Our flight brings us west across the United States to Seattle,
Washington. We begin the last leg of our trip far from the tropics in
Olympic National Park, where we will visit a temperate rainforest. At one
time, temperate rainforests were found on almost every continent. Half
of those that remain are here in North America. Temperate rainforests
occur in a narrow band between the ocean and the coastal mountains,
from Northern California to Alaska. Rainfall exceeds 80 inches (203.2 cm)
each year in these forests, and there are very few wildfires.

The temperate rainforest might seem quite unlike its tropical counterparts, but on closer look you'll find that there are many similarities. The first difference you will undoubtedly notice is the temperature. Let's see what other differences and similarities we can find in this Pacific Northwest rainforest.

Temperate Versus Tropical

Find the Pacific Northwest on a map and you will notice that it is much farther away from the equator than the tropical rainforests, which is why temperate rainforests are much cooler. What are some other differences between temperate and tropical rainforests? Looking around the temperate rainforest you will see that tree species are very different from those found in tropical rainforests. In the tropics we saw trees with very wide, broad leaves. In the temperate rainforest the canopy is filled with needle leaf trees. Remember the epiphytes? In the tropics we saw many orchid and fern epiphytes. Here we see epiphytes, but they are mostly lichens and mosses. Here's a new word for you: *biomass*. Tropical rainforests average about 300 tons (272 metric tons) of living biomass (a measurement of the total amount of living and dead material in an area) per acre (.4 ha), while temperate rainforests average about 500 tons (453 metric tons)—the most biomass of any ecosystem on the planet! However, tropical rainforests are much richer in biodiversity than temperate rainforests. Half of the world's known species of wildlife live in tropical rainforests. The biodiversity of the temperate rainforests is much lower—fewer varieties of creatures, but in greater numbers.

Where Are the Monkeys?

You won't hear the sounds of parrots or the screech of monkeys in a temperate rainforest, but you will hear the tweets and squawks of dark-eyed juncos, American dippers, gray jays, chestnut-backed chickadees, and, if you're lucky, northern spotted owls. The temperate rainforest is also home to a number of mammals, including black bears, cougars, bobcats, raccoons, deer, and elk. Some of these creatures have taken center stage in the fight for rainforest conservation. Perhaps the most well known and controversial is the northern spotted owl. Take a closer look.

Temperate Rainforests of the Pacific Northwest   95

Debate Whoooo Goes There

The northern spotted owl has created quite a commotion in the Pacific Northwest. Among owls, it is on the medium side, weighing about 1 to 1.6 pounds (.5 to .7 kg) with a length of 16 to 19 inches (41 to 48 cm). It

Northern Spotted Owl

is nocturnal, swooping down at night to feed on small mammals in the forest. Its low population of 3,000 to 5,000 pairs placed it in the "threatened" category of the Federal Threatened Species List in 1990, and it is protected under the Endangered Species Act. Both the Endangered Species Act and the Federal Threatened Species List were established by the government to help protect wildlife species from extinction. When a species is placed under their protection, laws are set in place to protect the species and its habitat. Because of this, the northern spotted owl has the unique ability to send shivers down the spine of any Northwest logger. There was a time when the only thought given to this area was for logging. The trees in much of the forest are well over 100 years old and are valuable to logging companies because of their size and the hardness of their wood. These include Douglas fir, redwood, and red and white cedar trees. By the early 1970s much of the area had already been overlogged. In fact, it had been reduced by over 85 percent. It was then that the northern spotted owl entered the picture. Battle lines were soon drawn between conservationists, who wanted to save the forests, a vital habitat for the owl, and loggers employed to cut down the forest. You probably could not have picked up a newspaper in the 1980s without seeing an article focusing on the owl.

In 1994, the Northwest Forest Plan was established to manage 17 old-growth forests in the Pacific Northwest. It said that the United States government must consider the effect that logging has on roughly 1,000 wildlife species of old-growth forests. That means that the U.S. Forest Service and the Bureau of Land Management has to conduct wildlife surveys of the species affected by logging in the forests. Without this plan, it's estimated that roughly 400 species would be at risk of extinction. The controversy is still an extremely sensitive subject in the Pacific Northwest. Use this activity to explore the tensions that exist between the loggers and the conservationists.

Have you ever watched a debate? A *debate* is a contest of ideas. A topic is chosen to debate and each side chooses a point of view to argue. Here's your chance to debate the points of view of the conservationists and the loggers over the plight of the northern spotted owl.

What You Need
- 2 or more friends
- Paper
- Pencil

What You Do
1. Divide your group up into two teams. Pick one person or some parents to serve as the judges of the debate. Decide which team will argue for the loggers and which team will argue for the conservationists.

2. Each group should make a list of all the points that are important to them. For example, the loggers might want to talk about the impact of government rules on their jobs, while the conservationists might want to talk about the importance of the owl to the environment. Check out some of the resources listed in the Rainforest Resources section to learn more about each side of this controversy.

3. Each team takes a few minutes to present its opening statement. Then the two teams take turns arguing their cases. The judges need to moderate the debate and make sure that each team gets the same amount of time to speak.

4. At the end of the debate, the judges determine which team was more successful in presenting its case.

The Amazing, Stupendous Yew Trees!

Northern spotted owls may have taken center stage, but the yew trees have acted as a terrific understudy. Yew trees are among the oldest in the world. In fact, there is a yew tree in Scotland that is reported to be 6,000 years old. Now that's old! Imagine what that tree has seen! There are also yew trees in the Pacific Northwest. They average anywhere from 200 to 400 years old. But yew trees are not making headlines because of

Yew branch

The yew tree is not the only rainforest plant that has been found to be medicinal. Tropical and temperate rainforests have a wealth of plant life that provide medicines, and maybe even cures for diseases yet to be discovered. For example, quinine, which is used to treat malaria, comes from the bark of several species of the rainforest tree *cinchona*. Another drug, called reserpine, is used to reduce high blood pressure and comes from the bark of a rainforest shrub called *rauvolfia*. People need these medicines to survive, but the rainforests throughout the world are in danger of extinction. What will we do with our own, right here in the United States?

their longevity. There's another reason. Taxol, a new, valuable, cancer-fighting drug, is derived from the bark of the yew tree. The problem is that it takes a lot of bark to produce a small amount of Taxol. Here's where the news headlines come into play. The yew tree is also home to the northern spotted owl. Conservationists are at work trying to preserve the yew trees in the Pacific Northwest, but scientists and many others are fighting to harvest the yew trees. Again we are in the same dilemma—do we save the rainforest or harvest a valuable medicine and provide jobs for loggers who need to feed their families? What do you think? This is another rainforest controversy that is great to debate with your friends and family.

How Old Are Yew?

As you have seen, yew trees can live a very long time. Can you imagine living as long as a yew tree? Take a look at the life of a Pacific yew that is 300 years old. Let's figure out some of the things that this yew tree has seen.

What You Need

🜲 Ruler

🜲 Pencil

🜲 Paper

What You Do

1. Make a line across your paper to create your time line. Write the current year on the far right end of the line. Subtract 300 from the current year and write that number at the far left end of the time line. Add the years for 200 and 100 years ago in the middle section of your time line.

2. Let's work backward from the present to add some dates to the time line. Start by putting the year you were born close to the left of the current year. Next, add the years your parents were born to the left of your birthday year, working your way backward on the time line. Add any other birthday years you know.

3. Here are some other dates you can add to your time line: 1912, when the Oreo cookie was invented; 1935, the year Elvis Presley was born; 1920, when women won the right to vote; 1865, when the Civil War ended; 1776, when the United States won its independence. See if you can add some others.

4. Look at your finished time line. Imagine living through all of those events. Perhaps you can even imagine the different people who might have walked past one of those yew trees during its lifetime. At one time, early in the yew's life, one of those people would have probably been a Native American from one of the Northwest tribes.

5. Here's an additional challenge for you. On the other side of your paper, draw a yew tree and one of the events it might have lived through.

The Redwood Forests

Northern California coastal rainforests boast majestic redwood trees that grow to unbelievable heights of 350 feet (106.7 m), making them the tallest trees in the United States and the world. They are able to reach those heights because they grow all year long in a climate that has a moderate average temperature of 60 degrees Fahrenheit (15 degrees Celsius) and up to 150 inches (381 cm) of rainfall each year. Redwood forests are located at the southernmost tip of the Pacific Northwest rainforests that extend from Alaska to Northern California. Unfortunately, only 4 percent of the original redwoods are still standing in the region. Some of these giant redwoods are ancient, reaching

Rainforest Reflection

Groups of environmentalists feel so strongly that the redwoods should not be cut down that they have taken up residence in the trees to protect them from the chainsaws. One activist, Julia Butterfly Harris, climbed up into a redwood named Luna and lived in the tree's branches for two years. You can learn more about the work of these tree sitters in the Rainforest Resources section. Do you think you would go that far to protect a tree from a chainsaw?

1,000 to 1,500 years old. Yet they remain in danger of being cut down by logging companies who supply wood for lumberyards, contractors, interior designers, and builders to make window frames, hot tubs, and decks, among other things. Read how you can help protect rainforest trees from logging in Chapter 10.

Make Your Own Totem Pole

Have you ever seen a totem pole? *Totem poles* are created as symbols of Native American families or clans of the Pacific Northwest and are often made from the wood of cedar trees. Like other rainforest people, the tribes of the Pacific Northwest incorporate the animals of the rainforest into their art. The totem poles they create tell stories and frequently depict bears and beavers. Each animal that is carved into the tree represents something. For example, the bear spirit represents the ability to work hard. For women, it symbolizes the ability to be a good mother; for men, the ability to be a successful hunter. The poles are usually painted with red, blue, green, black, and white paints. Here's a way for you to create your own personal totem pole that represents you.

TOTEM POLE ANIMALS

Animal	Meaning
Mountain Goat	Nobility
Grizzly Bear	Strength
Killer Whale	Ruler of the Seas
Beaver	Creativity
Bumblebee	Honesty
Dove	Love
Eagle	Great Strength
Owl	Wisdom
Raven	Knowledge
Seal	Inquisitive Nature
Otter	A Trusting Nature
Thunderbird	Mystery and Power

What You Need
- Paper (several sheets, to cover the length of the paper tube)
- Red, blue, green, white, and black markers
- White craft glue
- Wrapping paper tube

What You Do

1. Think about what type of animal describes you. What abilities do you have that an animal could represent? Use the chart to pick a few animals to represent you on your totem.

2. Next, draw the animal faces on your paper. The Native Americans use an egg shape for eyes and claws. They also frequently use U shapes in their totems. When you draw the animal faces, stack them so that they can be placed in a row on your totem pole.

3. Glue the paper onto the tube. Smooth it out so there are no bumps or air bubbles. Your finished totem pole is ready to display.

Beaver totem   Bear totem

The King and Queen of the Pacific Northwest

It has been said that for many, many years the forest was the king and the salmon was the queen of the Pacific Northwest. The forests of the Pacific Northwest were created eons ago by Mt. Rainier, named for British explorer Capt. George Vancouver's friend Peter Rainier; Mt. St. Helens, named for Vancouver's friend, Baron St. Helens; Mt. Baker, named after Lt. Joseph Baker, who sighted the mountain from Vancouver's boat *Discovery*; and other volcanoes, but the forest was also created by the salmon that swam through the forest's streams. How can a fish help create a forest? Well, many of the salmon perished in the streams, and like all creatures that die, they decomposed back into the ecosystem. In this way, the salmon brought nutrients from the ocean into the forests. They helped enrich the soil. Without them, the rainforest could not support such an abundance of life.

Salmon Migration

Pacific salmon hatch and live in the rainforest's freshwater streams. The adult salmon lays between 3,000 and 7,000 eggs. When the tiny fish hatch out of the egg they still have a bit of the egg with them in the form of a yolk sack that sticks out of them. The sack contains the protein, sugar, and minerals the tiny baby, called an *alevin*, needs to survive. Finally the sack disappears and the alevin turns into a *fingerling* that looks more like a tiny fish. The fingerlings then begin their long swim to the ocean to live as adults. On the way they get bigger and bigger. When they are mature, which can be any time between six months and seven years, they migrate back to the freshwater streams to spawn. How do they know where they started life? One theory is that they can smell their way home. The trip back to the streams where they were born is very stressful to the salmon. Some salmon actually have to travel 2,500 miles to reach their destination. They do not feed after they leave the ocean, so many die along the way. The ones that survive the long swim are often bruised and battered. Of the many that begin the migration each year, only a small percentage of them actually survive the full migration. They lay their eggs and begin the process all over again. Most adult salmon die soon after they lay their eggs.

Celebrate with a Potlatch

The Native Americans of the Pacific Northwest hold festivals called potlatches. These events are not just an ordinary party or fiesta. The potlatch can take a whole year to plan and is like a family reunion, except that during a potlatch, weddings and other celebrations are sometimes included. During the multi-day festivities there is dancing, feasting, and storytelling. You don't have to take a year to plan your own potlatch to celebrate the Pacific Northwest rainforest. Here are some tips to help you.

What You Need

- Invitations
- Small gifts or favors
- Plenty of great food
- Music for dancing
- Rainforest stories

What You Do

1. As with any party planning, the first item on the agenda is to pick a date to hold your potlatch and then invite your friends. It's a great idea to make your own invitations. Borrow some designs from your totem pole or other Pacific

Northwest native tribal designs to decorate your invitation. Look in the Rainforest Resources section for some Web sites that feature native tribal designs.

2. It is customary to give a favor or a gift to the people who attend your potlatch. Traditionally, Native Americans gave carved boxes, jewelry, canoes, blankets, oil, furniture, and other practical gifts. As times and needs have changed, the gifts have changed, too. They now include household items and toys for the children. Think about a small gift that you can give to your guests.

3. Plan your menu. The tribes hunted in the rainforests for elk, deer, roots, bracken fern, and huckleberries. They also ate salmon and shellfish. Those choices are probably not the best for your own potlatch, but you can be inspired by them to create your own menu. Perhaps you could serve potato or sweet potato chips or other root chips. How about setting out some bowls of local berries, both dried and fresh? What else do you think you could serve?

4. When your guests arrive, begin the event by giving a short speech welcoming everyone to the potlatch. When that is completed, put on your music, pull out some stories you have found (with the help of the Rainforest Resources section), and enjoy some yummy foods. Make sure to let your guests add their own stories and games to the festivities. Native American potlatches often included weddings and other celebrations, so celebrate recent birthdays, anniversaries, and the people you care about.

The Raven and the Potlatch: A Tale of the Pacific Northwest

The Native American tales of the Pacific Northwest often include the raven, a large relative of the crow. The raven is a trickster, just like the African trickster, Anansi. These tales are told by the tribe during a potlatch. The raven is often described as lazy and a bit mischievous.

Raven

Raven was lazy. He did not prepare for the cold winter months ahead like the other animals did, and he found himself cold and hungry when winter came. He started visiting some of the other animals for food and was turned away by each animal. Raven then went to visit his friend, Crow, and asked Crow about his upcoming potlatch. Crow had not planned a potlatch, but after Raven praised Crow's singing, Crow decided a potlatch would be a good time to show off his talent. While Crow sang and sang at the potlatch, Raven ate all of Crow's food and played host. Crow sang so much that at the end all he could do is caw, just as he does now. Raven was such a great host that, to this day, he gets invited to everyone's potlatches all winter. Of course, as you can see, Raven does not go hungry.

See if you can find other trickster tales told by other cultures in the folktale section of your library. After you read a few, try writing your own.

Time to Head Home

Well, our travels have come to an end. It's now time to head home. But that doesn't mean the adventure is over. Now it's time to find out what you can do at home to help the rainforests all over the world, and what other people are doing to help rainforest conservation. It's time for the real work to begin. Pack up your souvenirs and roll up your sleeves for what comes next.

10

DON'T BUNGLE THE JUNGLE

Well, it has been some trip, and now we're finally home. We discovered gorillas in Africa, butterflies in the Amazon, bats in Asia, and so many other creatures all over the world. We saw the effects of logging in the Pacific Northwest, the results of deforestation in Borneo, and the endangerment of many species in Hawaii. Now it's time to figure out what we can do to help rainforests in our own country and throughout the world. It's also a great time to look at what other groups and individuals are doing to help preserve these important ecosystems.

Boardwalk Repairs Endanger Rainforest

In 2001, a New Jersey Superior Court judge issued an *injunction*, which is an order to stop work, blocking the town of Asbury Park from making some much-needed repairs to its famous boardwalk. Why all the commotion about a New Jersey boardwalk? After all, there are no rainforests in New Jersey. Well, the repairs were to be made with a wood called *ipe* (pronounced EE-pay), which is a tropical hardwood that grows in the Brazilian rainforest. The group Rainforest Relief claimed that the boardwalk repairs would require so much wood that 30,000 acres of Brazilian rainforest would be devastated. The group later lost their lawsuit and construction of the boardwalk was set to begin. Fortunately, the sides reached an agreement to use recycled rainforest hardwood rather than wood from living trees. The recycled wood comes from dead trees that have been underwater in a flooded area in the rainforest. Years before, the area had been flooded by an artificial dam that was built to create a lake. Rainforest Relief called the agreement a victory.

More About Ipe

Ipe is an emergent tree that can live to be 300 years old and even possibly up to 1,000 years old. Only one or two trees grow in an acre (.4 ha), so when the area is logged for these trees, many other kinds of trees are also cut down. Not all the other trees end up being used. For an area the size of Asbury Park's boardwalk, up to 10,000 trees would need to be cut down for every 100,000 feet (30,480 m) of the boardwalk.

Help Save Tropical Hardwoods

Many types of wood that are used in the United States and elsewhere come from the rainforest. Mahogany and ipe are just two of them. Ipe can be found at lumberyards and home centers, where it is frequently bought by contractors for home decks and outdoor benches. Mahogany is used for furniture and coffins. Here are some things you can do to help save these hardwoods.

- Logging in rainforests displaces the natives from their homes, causes animal species to become endangered or extinct, and contributes to global warming. You can help by telling people about these rainforest woods and why it is bad to log in the rainforests.

- Find out if local home centers or lumberyards carry ipe or other rainforest hardwoods. If they do, you can write the home center or lumberyard a letter telling them about the problems logging causes and asking them to stop carrying the wood.

- You can also write a letter to your local newspaper.
- You can also write a letter to your representative in Congress and to your senator.

No matter what you decide to do, be sure to get a parent involved.

Slow Down Global Warming

Scientists have been studying the global warming of our planet. *Global warming* is the increase in the average temperature of our planet. If the temperature rises, the icebergs in the arctic begin to melt and raise the water level in the oceans. There are other problems as well. Intense rainstorms are a result of global warming, and so is a decrease in soil moisture, which affects farming. Scientists have discovered that *deforestation*, or the cutting down of all the trees of the rainforest, is a contributing factor to global warming. Some countries use the slash-and-burn method of clearing the forest. *Slash and burn* means that the vegetation is cut down and then it is burned. This risky, sometimes uncontrollable method of clearing land not only destroys a tremendous amount of wildlife, but the fires produce a large amount of carbon dioxide, methane, ozone, and nitrous oxide. These gases are known as greenhouse gases. *Greenhouse gases* are gases that trap heat in the atmosphere and cause global warming. Deforestation contributes to global warming because it removes one of the Earth's ways to absorb the extra carbon dioxide in the atmosphere. Trees absorb and store carbon from the atmosphere through photosynthesis. Fewer trees mean less carbon is removed from the atmosphere, and our earth's temperature continues to rise.

There is still time to make a difference. Here are some things you can do to help.

- You can plant trees in your community to help combat global warming. Every tree makes a difference.
- Help decrease the amount of greenhouse gases that are released into our atmosphere by decreasing the amount of energy you use. When we burn fossil fuels such as oil to heat our houses, we release greenhouse gases. Talk to your parents about keeping your thermostat lower in the winter and higher in the summer.
- Our cars release greenhouse gases. Use public transportation, bicycles, or walk instead of driving.
- It takes energy to make the packaging we use. Packaging includes plastic wrap and paper or plastic containers. Think about what you buy when you go shopping with your parents. Shop for items that use less packaging.
- Recycle as much as you can. Also look for and purchase items that use recycled materials.
- Support organizations that are working on researching and combating global warming.

Trading in Parrots Means Big Business

Walk into any pet shop and you're bound to see a parrot or two for sale. Do you know where that parrot came from? Was it bred for the pet industry, or was it captured from its native rainforest in Africa or South America? Well, until recently, most of the birds in pet shops were captured in the wild. This is still the case in many other countries around the world. In fact, between the years of 1997 and 2000, the European Union imported more than 460,000 wild birds. These birds do not make good pets and usually are not cared for properly. Not only do the parrot populations decrease as a result of deforestation of the rainforest, the parrots that survive are then threatened with capture for the pet market. As discussed in Chapter 6, statistics show that, on average, for every bird that is captured and completes its journey, another 10 die during capture or in transit.

On a good note, the state of New York banned the import of wild birds in 1984, and in 1992 the United States passed the Wild Bird Conservation Act to promote the conservation of wild exotic birds. At the time the Conservation Act was passed, the United States was the largest importer of rainforest birds caught in the wild. Since the Act was passed, the pet bird trade in the United States has increased. Now, commercial breeders raise birds for the pet trade. Birds bred in captivity are healthier and tamer than birds caught in the wild and therefore make much better pets.

That is the good side of the story. Wild birds are still being caught and sold for the European and Asian markets. Let's find out what you can do to help.

Wild Bird Trade: Here's How You Can Help

When trading is going on between countries so far away it's difficult to see how you can help from your home, but there are things you can do.

- Learn more about the proper care of birds. Tell others about what you learn.
- It's fun to see birds in restaurants and stores, but take a close look at the care of these birds. If you see that the bird is not properly cared for, tell a grown-up to report the case to the owner of the business or the local Humane Society.
- Participate in a program that purchases rainforest land for conservation. The Tropical Rainforest Coalition and the Rainforest Alliance are just two of the organizations that sponsor such programs. Check out the Rainforest Resources section for some others.
- Hold a community car wash or other fundraiser to raise funds to purchase rainforest land. Display posters about the rainforest at your fundraiser. Make one that shows all the different species of parrots and educates people about the bird trade.

Rainforest Reflection

Large parrots can live up to 70 or 80 years, which means that they are a big investment. Because of their long lifespan, parrots are usually passed from owner to owner. This can be a very unpleasant way for a wild bird to live. Imagine such a bird living free among wild orchids and green trees, then facing the next 50 or more years in a cage. Does living in a cage for this long sound inviting? In addition to living in a cage for that long, these birds usually end up having many owners over the course of their lives, because either their owners can't take care of them for such a long time or the owner dies and leaves the bird to someone else.

Activist Offers Borneo Government $10,000

In 2000, Bruno Manser, a rainforest activist who had lived with the Penan in Borneo, offered the government of Borneo $10,000 to help the Penan. The Penan just might be the last nomadic rainforest tribe left, and their conditions have grown worse with the increase of logging in Borneo. The government in Borneo wants to take them out of the rainforest and give them homes, schools, and work. The Penan want to remain in their home, the rainforest, where they have lived for centuries. The government turned down Manser's offer, calling it a publicity stunt. Manser lived with the Penan until his arrest in 1987 for anti-logging activities. The Penan continue to struggle for their land. Manser is still working for the people of the rainforest through his organization, Bruno–Manser–Fronds Society for the Peoples of the Rainforest.

The Penan are only one tribe fighting desperately to remain in the rainforests. There are others in Africa, South America, and elsewhere that have always believed that land could not be owned, only borrowed. These people, like all the other creatures of the rainforests, might soon become endangered. Can you imagine living in a rainforest tribe? How would you feel if your forest and home were cut down and you had to move? Perhaps you can compare these tribes with the Native Americans who were forcibly removed from their native lands and placed on reservations.

Help Save the Rainforest Tribes

A number of organizations are trying to help the rainforest natives. One group is the Rainforest Foundation. You can find their Web site and contact information in the Rainforest Resources section. Rainforest tribes need our support and assistance to keep them free and living in their rainforests. Here are some other things you can do to help.

Rainforest Reflection
The population of native peoples in Brazil was once six million. However, with the destruction of the rainforest for developing roads, buildings, and agriculture, the population has declined to about 200,000. Can you figure out how much of this population has declined and express it as a percentage? The total population of Brazil is 172.8 million people. What percentage of the total population are the native peoples?

- Support other groups that are working for the people of the rainforest. Share information about these groups with people you know. Tell your friends and teachers about the people of the rainforest and their struggle for existence.
- Learn about the different tribes of the rainforests. Look in the Rainforest Resources section for some books that will tell you more about these people. The more you know, the more you can help. Part of the problem is that many people do not know the tribes of the rainforests and the problems they face. People can only help once they understand.
- Investigate programs that help the people of the rainforest. The POLE (Pollution Offset Lease for Earth) Project is one example of a project that enables tribes to live in the rainforest and protect it. It recognizes the benefits of the rainforest in providing oxygen, water, habitats, and soil, among other things, and the ability of the tribes to become the caretakers of the rainforest. Look at the Rainforest Resources section for more information.
- Buy crafts and other products that help sustain the tribe's natural way of life. The sale of seed necklaces and tagua buttons provide tribes with necessary money, and these items are harvested without harming the rainforest. Check out other items that are offered for sale in our country.

Looking Toward the Future

There are always new challenges to rainforest preservation and new opportunities to help. Check out the Rainforest Resources section for organizations that are working to help the rainforest ecosystems throughout the world. Their Web sites will have updates on specific rainforests and offer ways that you can help. Check them often and keep yourself informed about these truly marvelous places on Earth.

RAINFOREST RESOURCES

Favorite Books, Videos, and Web Sites

CHAPTER 1: THE FOREST FLOOR

Books

Cole, Joanna. *The Magic School Bus Meets the Rot Squad: A Book About Decomposition.* New York: Scholastic, 1995.

Courlander, Harold. *A Treasury of African Folklore.* New York: Marlowe & Co., 1996.

Kimmel, Eric. *Anansi and the Moss-Covered Rock.* New York: Holiday House, 1988.

Lavies, Bianca. *Compost Critters.* New York: Dutton, 1993.

McDermott, Gerald. *Anansi, the Spider.* New York: Henry Holt & Co., Inc., 1987.

Web Sites

Take a look at all the different rainforest layers, starting with the forest floor, at this Web site.
www.pbs.org/tal/costa_rica/layers.html

Learn about composting from the Science Museum of Minnesota.
www.smm.org/sln/tf/w/worms/worms/compost.html

Learn about the Worm Compost Project by Museum Magnet School in St. Paul, Minnesota.
www.sci.mus.mn.us/sln/tf/w/worms/worms/worms.html

See the Theraphosa blondi and other tarantulas at Tarantulas.com.
www.tarantulas.com

Check out this Web site to see pictures of fruiting fungi.
http://mycor.nancy.inra.fr/about/gallery2

CHAPTER 2: THE UNDERSTORY

Books

Saint-Exupéry, Antoine de. *The Little Prince.* New York: Harcourt, Brace & World, 1943.

Yolen, Jane. *Welcome to the Green House.* New York: Putnam's and Sons, 1993.

Web Sites

See a list of tropical houseplants at the New York Botanical Garden.
www.nybg.org/plants/factsheets/tropical.html

Check out the rainforest plant photos at GreenDealer.
www.greendealer-exotic-seeds.com/seeds/RainForest.html

Listen to rainforest sounds at these two sites.
www.christiananswers.net/kids/sounds.html
www.exploratorium.edu/frogs/rainforest

Learn more about boa constrictors at the Belize Zoo.
www.belizezoo.org

Check out photographs of rainforest snakes at this Web site.
www.greentreesnakes.com

CDs

Peter, Paul and Mommy (by the musical group Peter, Paul,
and Mary), WEA/Warner Bros., original release 1969, CD
release 1990.

CHAPTER 3: THE CANOPY

Shopping

Looking for your very own bromeliad or airplant to grow at
home? You can find inexpensive plants at local garden
centers. Most cost under five dollars.

Web Sites

View a variety of beautiful orchids at Brazilian Orchids.
www.delfinadearaujo.com/showroom/showroom.htm

CHAPTER 4: AT THE TOP

Books

Himmelman, John. *A Hummingbird's Life*. New York:
Scholastic Library, 2000.

Kalman, Bobbie D. *Rainforest Birds*. Ontario, Canada:
Crabtree Publishing Co., 1997.

Web Sites

Take a look at some photos of native people from the Pacific
dressed in ceremonial bird masks.
www.abc.net.au/arts/artok/bodyart/body_art_png1.htm

Check out World Bird Festival for information on bird lore,
national birds, and native uses of bird feathers.
www.birdlife.net/festival

Look at hummingbird migration maps.
www.hummingbirds.net

CHAPTER 5: JOURNEY TO AFRICA

Books

Brown, Don. *Uncommon Traveler: Mary Kingsley in Africa*.
New York: Houghton Mifflin, 2000.

Olaleye, Isaac. *Bitter Bananas*. Honesdale, PA: Boyds Mills
Press, 1994.

Olaleye, Isaac. *Lake of the Big Snake: An African Rainforest
Adventure*. Honesdale, PA: Boyds Mills Press, 1998.

Videos

Reader's Digest Presents The Enchanted Island: Madagascar.
ABC/KANE Productions International, 1998.

Web Sites

Check out these Web sites for information about Tarzan.
www.tarzan.org
www.ac.wwu.edu/~stephan/Tarzan

The Columbus Zoo's Mountain Gorilla Veterinary Project will give you many opportunities to view gorillas and other creatures of the African rainforest.
www.colszoo.org

Here's Koko's Kid's Club. Find out all about the gorilla named Koko who learned to speak in sign language.
www.koko.org/kidsclub

The African Wildlife Foundation is devoted to conserving the wildlife of Africa. Get a view of many of Africa's creatures and how you can help them.
www.awf.org

Check out the recipes at the Web site for *The Congo Cookbook.*
www.congocookbook.com

Take a look at the International String Figure Association.
www.isfa.org

Find out how children are named in Ghana.
www.experiment.org

Get your mood rings here.
www.moodjewelry.com

CHAPTER 6: SOUTH AMERICAN JUNGLES

Books

Baker, Jeanne. *Where the Forest Meets the Sea.* New York: Greenwillow, 1988.

Burleigh, Robert. *Chocolate Riches from the Rainforest.* New York: Harry N. Abrams, Inc., 2002.

Cherry, Lynn. *The Great Kapok Tree.* New York: Harcourt, 1990.

Cherry, Lynn and Mark Plotkin. *The Shaman's Apprentice.* New York: Harcourt, 1998.

Goodman, Susan E. *Ultimate Field Trip Adventures in the Amazon Rainforest.* New York: Aladdin, 1999.

Roosevelt, Theodore. *Through the Brazilian Wilderness.* New York: Charles Scribner's Sons, 1924.

Videos

Reader's Digest Presents The Living Edens: Amazon's Manu. ABC/Kane Productions International, 1997.

Web Sites

See pictures of and learn about rainforest animals, plants, and people at this Web site.
www.junglephotos.com

Check out the World Wildlife Fund Web site for information, beautiful pictures, and even the sounds of the rainforest and its many creatures.
www.worldwildlife.org

Find out more about the butterfly discoveries of the 2001 expedition by American scientists Jason Hall and Keith Willmott.
www.purplemountain.com

Take the sloth quiz and test your sloth knowledge.
www.geocities.com/Hollywood/Set/1478/quiz.html

Here's the Web site for Butterfly World. Learn all about the butterfly gardens at this great spot located in Tradewinds Park, Florida. Even if you can't visit the park, the site has plenty of information about butterflies.
www.butterflyworld.com

The Butterfly Farm is another great site. Take a look at the butterflies from Costa Rica. You might even plan a visit.
www.butterflyfarm.co.cr

See photos and hear sounds of the rainforests in Costa Rica and Guatemala.
www.rainforesteducation.com

See how chocolate is made.
www.hersheys.com

Get more information about chocolate here.
www.fmnh.org/Chocolate/about.html

Look in natural food stores for Glee Gum, made with chicle, or buy it from Jungle Gum.
www.junglegum.com/Chicle/chicle.html

Check out the Seed Project. Learn more about this program to help the Shuar people of South America.
www.dreamchange.org/projects/seed.html

Check out Children of the Amazon. Look at the rainforest through the eyes of kids who live there.
www.ccph.com/cota

Here you'll find some great photographs of the Amazon.
www.junglephotos.com

CHAPTER 7: SOUTH ASIAN AND MALAYSIAN RAINFORESTS

Books

Kipling, Rudyard. *The Jungle Book*. London: Pavilion Classics, 1997.
This is one of the many editions available.

Videos

Walt Disney's The Jungle Book. Disney, 1994.

In the Wild: Orangutans with Julia Roberts. PBS Home Video, 1998.

Web Sites

Learn more about the Eco Challenge in Borneo.
www.ecochallenge.com/borneo

Take a look at some pictograms.
www.piktogramm.com

See the orangutans at the Smithsonian Think Tank.
www.smithsonianmag.si.edu/smithsonian/issues96/jun96/think.html

See some Wayang klitik puppets here.
www.geocities.com/murnijava/central_javapuppets.htm
www.sbcss.k12.ca.us/sbcss/services/educational/cctechnology/webquest/puppetry.html

Batik is a beautiful Indonesian craft. Take a look at some examples.
http://discover-indo.tierranet.com/batikpag.htm

CHAPTER 8: ISLAND RAINFORESTS OF THE PACIFIC AND CARIBBEAN

Books

Lee, Alfonso Silva. *Coqui and His Friends.* St. Paul, MN: Pangaea Press, 2000.

Web Sites

Check out this great site about Hawaii.
http://coy.ne.client2.attbi.com/HAWAII-GS.html

Check out the meanings of Hawaiian flowers.
www.flowervr.com/Aloha/alohablends.htm

Print out pictures of Hawaii's endangered species to color from the state of Hawaii's Division of Forestry and Wildlife.
www.state.hi.us/dlnr/dofaw/kids/endgrbk

Learn more about Hawaii's endangered species.
www.hisurf.com/~enchanted

Find out more about Puerto Rico and its rainforest in the BoricuaKids section.
www.elboricua.com

Read sound poems from different authors at these Web sites.
http://home.earthlink.net/~barleydog/WORDSOUNDCOMP OSITIONS.html
www.gigglepoetry.com/poetryclass/soundhelp.html

Help the effort to save bats with Bat Conservation International.
www.batcon.org

CHAPTER 9: TEMPERATE RAINFORESTS OF THE PACIFIC NORTHWEST

Books

Frantz, Jennifer. *Totem Poles.* New York: Grosset & Dunlap, 2001.

Hill, Julia Butterfly. *The Legacy of Luna: The Story of a Tree, a Woman and the Struggle to Save the Redwoods.* San Francisco: Harper, 2001.

Hoyt-Goldsmith, Diane. *Totem Pole.* New York: Holiday House, 1990.

Geisel, Theodore (Dr. Seuss). *The Lorax.* New York: Random House, 1971.

Okimoto, Jean Davies. *No Dear, Not Here: The Marbeled Murrelets' Quest for a Nest in the Pacific Northwest.* Seattle, WA: Sasquatch Books, 1995.

Web Sites

Find some fun Pacific Northwest activities here.
http://192.211.16.13/n/nadkarnn/TRFwebsite/TRFhome.htm

The Yew Tree Debate: Check out some roles you can play in a debate over the yew trees.
www.chemheritage.org/EducationalServices/pharm/chemo/activity/debate.htm

Learn more about the fate of trees in the United States and what you can do to help at American Forests.
www.americanforests.org

Take a look at these totem poles.
www.nativewoodart.com/totem.html

CHAPTER 10: DON'T BUNGLE THE JUNGLE

Books

Pringle, Laurence P. *Global Warming*. New York: Sea Star Books, 2001.

Vriends, Matthew M. *Simon & Schuster's Guide to Pet Birds*. New York: Simon & Schuster, 1984.

Wellner, Pamela and Eugene Dickey. *Rainforest Action Network Wood User Guide*. New York: Rainforest Action Network, 1991.

Web Sites

Learn about the POLE (Pollution Offset Lease for Earth) Project.
www.dreamchange.org/programs/pole.html

Adopt a primate from the Duke University Primate Center. Lemurs from Madagascar and other primates need your support. As a sponsor for a year, you can help with conservation efforts to help these special creatures. For more information call (919) 489-3364.
www.duke.edu/web/primate

Join Greenpeace's "Kid's for Forests" program. Greenpeace provides many online ways to help ancient forests.
www.greenpeaceusa.org/forests

At this Web site you can read the Wild Bird Conservation Act for yourself.
http://international.fws.gov/wbca/wbcaindx.html

Rainforest Organizations

National Wildlife Federation
11100 Wildlife Center Drive
Reston, VA 20190
(800) 822-9919
www.nwf.org
A large, member-supported conservation group designed to educate, inspire, and assist individuals and organizations of diverse cultures to protect the environment and preserve wildlife.

Rainforest Action Network
221 Pine Street, Suite 500
San Francisco, CA 94104
(415) 398-4404
www.ran.org
RAN works to protect tropical rainforests and the human rights of those living in and around those forests since 1985.

Rainforest Alliance
665 Broadway, Suite 500
New York, NY 10012
(212) 677-1900
www.rainforest-alliance.org
This is a leading international conservation organization that is focused on protecting ecosystems and the people and wildlife that live within them by implementing better business practices that facilitate biodiversity and sustainability.

Rainforest Foundation
270 Lafayette Street, Suite 1107
New York, NY 10012
(212) 431-9098
www.savetherest.org
The Rainforest Foundation's mission is to support native peoples and traditional populations of the rainforest in their efforts to protect their environment and their rights.

Tropical Rainforest Coalition
21730 Stevens Creek Boulevard, Suite 102
Cupertino, CA 95014
www.rainforest.org
This organization sponsors the Save-an-Acre program. For over 10 years it has worked to preserve tropical rainforest ecosystems and their native peoples and cultures.

Keep up with author Nancy Castaldo at her website: www.nancycastaldo.com

Places to Visit in the United States

Ready to travel to a rainforest? Speak to a tour guide or check out some informative sites on the Internet, such as Redjellyfish.com (www.redjellyfish.com) for expert advice. Make sure you prepare well in advance for any adventure vacation with your family.

Rainforest Cafe
www.rainforestcafe.com
This restaurant chain has locations nationwide. Get a feel for the rainforest by dining here.

ALABAMA

Birmingham Zoo
2630 Cahaba Road
Birmingham, AL 35223
(205) 879-0409
www.birminghamzoo.com
See the tropical rainforest exhibit and the alligator swamp.

CALIFORNIA

Chaffee Zoo of Fresno
894 W. Belmont Avenue
Fresno, CA 93728
(559) 498-2671
www.chaffeezoo.org
See the South American rainforest exhibit.

Santa Ana Zoo at Prentice Park
1801 E. Chestnut Avenue
Santa Ana, CA 92701
(714) 835-7484
http://santaanazoo.org
Tour the Colors of the Amazon, Amazon's Edge, Rainforest, and Life in the Treetops exhibits. You can also learn firsthand about rainforest destruction caused by the slash-and-burn method.

COLORADO

Cheyenne Mountain Zoological Society
4250 Cheyenne Mountain Zoo Road
Colorado Springs, CO 80906
(719) 633-9925
www.cmzoo.org
Check out the annual summer butterfly experience.

FLORIDA

Caribbean Gardens
1590 Goodlette-Frank Road
Naples, FL 34102
(941) 262-5409
www.napleszoo.com
Board a guided catamaran for a primate expedition cruise through nine islands inhabited by monkeys, lemurs, and apes.

Disney's Animal Kingdom
Off Interstate 4, west of the Florida Turnpike
Lake Buena Vista, FL 32830
(407) 824-4321
www.disney.ca/vacations/disneyworld

Tour the Asia exhibit for a look at Asian rainforests where bats with six-foot wingspans fly and tigers roam. Take a ride to Conservation Station and learn more about rainforest creatures. See gorillas in Africa.

GEORGIA

Zoo Atlanta
800 Cherokee Avenue SE
Atlanta, GA 30315
(888) 945-5432
www.zooatlanta.org
Visit the Ford African Rainforest exhibit, the Sumatran Tiger Forest exhibit, or the Asian Forest exhibit to see great examples of different rainforest ecosystems.

HAWAII

Hawaii Rainforest Zoo
Stainback Highway
Hilo, HI 96720
Or contact:
Friends of the Zoo
Box 738
Keaau, Hawaii 96749
www.hilozoo.com
Visit the only zoo in the United States that is in a rainforest.

Waikamoi Preserve
Haleakala National Park, via Highways 377 and 378
P.O. Box 1716
Makawao, Maui, Hawaii 96768
(808) 572-7849
http://ice.ucdavis.edu/~robyn/waikamoi.html
This wonderful 5,230-acre preserve is run by the Nature Conservancy. Check out the Web site for directions. Access is by guided hikes only.

ILLINOIS

Lincoln Park Zoo
2200 N. Cannon Drive
Chicago, IL 60614
(312) 742-2000
ww.lpzoo.com
This is a great, *free* zoo that offers you four trails of exhibits, including a great ape house, a primate house, and a bird house.

INDIANA

Fort Wayne Children's Zoo
3411 Sherman Boulevard
Fort Wayne, IN 46808
(260) 427-6800
www.kidszoo.com
In the zoo's Indonesian Rainforest Exhibit, you'll see butterflies, orangutans, Sumatran tigers, and many other rainforest critters.

Indianapolis Zoo
1200 W. Washington Street
Indianapolis, IN 46222
(317) 630-2001
www.indyzoo.com
Lemurs and other Madagascar critters are a must-see here.

KENTUCKY

Louisville Zoo
1100 Trevilian Way
Louisville, KY 40213
(502) 459-2181
www.louisvillezoo.org
Ride on Morphis, a simulator ride with changing shows, including one about a gorillas of the Virunga Mountains.

NEW YORK

The Bronx Zoo
Fordham Road and the Bronx River Parkway
Bronx, NY 10460
(718) 367-1010
Or Contact:
The Wildlife Conservation Society
2300 Southern Boulevard
Bronx, New York 10460
(718) 220-5100
www.bronxzoo.com
The Congo exhibit is a must-see, but plan enough time to see everything else, too.

The American Museum of Natural History
Central Park & 79th Street
New York, NY 10024
(212) 313-7278
www.amnh.org
The Dzanga-Sangh Rainforest, in the Hall of Biodiversity, is a must-see exhibit here.

OHIO

Cincinnati Zoo and Botanical Garden
3400 Vine Street
Cincinnati, OH 45220
(800) 94-HIPPO
www.cincyzoo.org
Check out the zoo's Jungle Trails, with rainforest critters from Asia and Africa, as well as Gorilla World, Monkey Island, and many other great rainforest exhibits.

OREGON

Oregon Zoo
4001 SW Canyon Road
Portland, Oregon 97221
(503) 220-2786
www.zooregon.org
The zoo's exhibits focus on African rainforests, the Amazon, Alaska, primates, and more.

PENNSYLVANIA

The Pittsburgh Zoo and Aquarium
1 Wild Place
Pittsburgh, PA 15206
(800) 474-4966
http://zoo.pgh.pa.us
Visit the zoo's Tropical Forest Complex, which houses more than 90 primates, including gorillas, orangutans, and tamarins.

SOUTH CAROLINA

Riverbanks Zoo and Botanical Garden
500 Wildlife Parkway
Columbia, SC 29202
(803) 779-8717
www.riverbanks.org
Visit the Ndoki Forest exhibit at this zoo.

TEXAS

Dallas Zoo
550 S. R.L Thornton Freeway (I-35E)
Dallas, TX 75203
(214) 670-5656
www.dallas-zoo.org
See the primates, tigers, and other creatures of Southeast Asia and Africa in the ExxonMobil Endangered Tiger Habitat and the Kimberly-Clark Chimpanzee Forest.

WASHINGTON

Hoodsport Ranger Station
150 N. Lake Cushman Road
Hoodsport, WA 98548
(360) 877-5254

Northwest Trek Wildlife Park
11610 Trek Drive East
Eatonville, WA 98328
(360) 832-6117
www.nwtrek.org

Olympic National Park
Hoh Rainforest Visitor Center
18113 Upper Hoh Road
Forks, Washington 98331
(360) 374-6925
www.nps.gov/olym

Olympic National Park Visitor Center
600 E. Park Avenue
Port Angeles, WA 98362
(360) 565-3132
www.portangeles.org/36.html

The National Parks of the Pacific Northwest are your gateway into the rainforests of this region.

WASHINGTON, DC

Smithsonian National Zoological Park
3001 Connecticut Avenue
Washington, DC 20008
http://natzoo.si.edu

Visit the park's Think Tank, Amazonia Exhibit, Great Ape House, and Great Cats exhibits. Check out the Web site for animal cams positioned around the park.

International Rainforest Experiences

AUSTRALIA

Queensland

Rainforest Habitat Wildlife Sanctuary
Port Douglas Road
Port Douglas, Queensland 4871
07 4099 3235
www.rainforesthabitat.com.au
The Rainforest Habitat boasts over 1,600 animals. There are guided tours, displays, and innovative immersion exhibits.

CANADA

Montreal

Montreal Biodôme
4777 Pierre-De Coubertin Avenue
Montréal, Québec, H1V 1B3
(514) 868-3000
www2.ville.montreal.qc.ca/biodome

The Tropical Forest ecosystem at the Biodôme is designed to replicate the South American rainforest.

Toronto

Toronto Zoo
361A Old Finch Avenue
Scarborough, Ontario M1B 5K7
Canada
(416) 392-5863
www.torontozoo.com
Visit the new Australasia Pavilion and the Gorilla Rainforest exhibit.

CARRIBEAN

Dominican Republic

Punta Cana Resort and Club
(888) 442-2262
www.puntacana.com
Designed with conservation in mind, this resort has a limited negative impact on the environment. In addition, the resort maintains organic vegetable and spice gardens, has formed the Punta Can Ecological Foundation, and has created a nature reserve. A joint venture with Cornell University involves research on native plants and organisms at the Punta Cana/Cornell Biodiversity Lab.

CENTRAL AMERICA

Panama

Gamboa Rainforest Resort
(877) 800-1690
www.gamboaresort.com
This resort features many rainforest exhibits, including the Reptiles & Amphibians Conservation and Ecology Exhibit. Visitors can explore the rainforest canopy of the Soberania National Park in the Gamboa Aerial Tram. In cooperation with the Smithsonian Tropical Research Institute, the resort also sponsors a number of ecological tours.

Rainforest Events Calendar

FEBRUARY
Hummingbirds can be seen in the southern Gulf Coast states on their northern migration.

APRIL

April 22

Earth Day
Check out the Earth Day Network for more information and ways to celebrate at www.earthday.net.

Last Friday in April

Plant a tree to celebrate Arbor Day. For more tips on celebrating the holiday check the National Arbor Day Foundation Web site at www.arborday.org/arborday/celebrate.html.

MAY

May 1

Lei Day

For more information about Lei Day, check out the Maui activity site at www.maui-activities.com/mayday.htm, or the Hula Pages at www.geocities.com/~olelo/mayday.html. Also check out the lei activity in Chapter 8.

AUGUST

Early August

Celebrate with an African Yam Festival, like the people do in early August in the countries of Ghana and Nigeria.

OCTOBER

Third week of October

World Rainforest Week

NOVEMBER

Orangutan Awareness Week

Check the Orangutan Foundation International Web site for annual event dates at www.orangutan.org/home/calendar.php.

Monarch Butterflies arrive in Mexico after migrating from the North.

DECEMBER

For the holidays, think about some green gift ideas, such as making a donation to one of the rainforest preservation organizations listed in this resource section, making a craft from this book and giving it as a gift, or adopting a rainforest animal. Below are examples of some of the organizations that feature adoption programs. In addition, many of the zoos listed in the resource section also provide adoption programs.

Adopt a Lemur

Duke Primate Center
3075 Erwin Road
Durham, NC 27705
(919) 489-3364
www.duke.edu/web/primate/adopt.html

Adopt a Gorilla

The Dian Fossey Gorilla Fund International
www.gorillafund.org

RAINFOREST CHALLENGES

CHAPTER 1

The Forest Floor

If you find a dead spider or have access to a preserved spider specimen, place it on a microscope slide and look at it through a microscope. Use a high power to view the foot of your spider. You will most likely see hairs. These hairs are for sensing sounds and movement. Take a closer look. Do you see claws? If you find hooked claws on the foot of the spider, then you know that your spider is a web-making spider. It uses the claws to hold on to the web. If you don't see claws it is most likely a jumping spider that hunts its prey and does not make webs.

CHAPTER 2

The Understory

Go outside on a dark night with two flowers—a red carnation and a white carnation. Place each one on a tree branch. Ask a friend to find the flowers. Which one was easier to find?

CHAPTER 3

The Canopy

Look at a world map. Find the following countries on the map: Belize, Brazil, Colombia, Costa Rica, Ecuador, Guatemala, Hong Kong, Panama, Singapore, Venezuela, and the Cayman Islands. All of these countries have designated the orchid as their national flower. What do these countries all have in common? Do they all have rainforests?

CHAPTER 4

At the Top

Hummingbirds can flap their wings faster than we can see. Can you find out how many times a hummingbird can flap its wings in a single second? Multiply what you find by 60 and you'll know how many times a hummingbird flaps its wings in a minute. Flap your arms as many times as you can in one minute. How do you compare with the hummingbird?

CHAPTER 5

Journey to Africa

Watch *Walt Disney's Tarzan*, *Disney's Tarzan & Jane*, or another movie that takes place in a rainforest and write down all of the animals you see. Compare your list to a list of animals that actually live in the rainforest. How many do you find on both lists?

CHAPTER 6

South American Jungles

New World monkeys are defined as the monkeys that inhabit the Americas. *Old World* monkeys inhabit Asia and Africa. There's a big difference between them. Can you find out what it is? Hint: It has to do with the tail.

CHAPTER 7

South Asian and Malaysian Rainforests

⚘ I'm Going to Borneo

Take out a backpack and try to pack it with the items that you named in the game on page 70. Does it all fit? If you brought canned food, did you remember a can opener? Did you remember insect repellent and first aid supplies?

⚘ Message Sticks

See how many pictograms you can find around your community. You might see pictograms that represent handicapped parking, restrooms, or no smoking. Make a list of some other ones that you find.

CHAPTER 8

Island Rainforests of the Pacific and Caribbean

⚘ Aliens Are Not from Outer Space

Create a house of cards. See how many cards you can stack before your deck falls. Like the rainforest ecosystem, a house of cards depends on all of the cards being in the right positions. If you take one card out, the whole house will crumble.

⚘ Mongoose on the Loose

The mongoose was brought to the Hawaiian Islands to get rid of the rats. Turn to page 88 to find out how the rats got to Hawaii.

CHAPTER 9

Temperate Rainforests of the Pacific Northwest

Draw a picture of a tropical rainforest and another picture of a temperate rainforest. Include the different trees that inhabit each rainforest layer and the critters that live in each layer.

CHAPTER 10

Don't Bungle the Jungle

Set up a recycling program at your school if there isn't already one. See if you can put a bin in the faculty room to collect cans and bottles. Donate the money you get when you recycle these to a rainforest organization.

INDEX

> "Using fun activities and games, *Oceans* brilliantly underscores the stewardship that kids have with the oceans."
>
> —Barbara Jeanne Polo, executive director, American Oceans Campaign

> "She delights in looking at the ocean from myriad viewpoints and children will enjoy her multifaceted sensibility."
>
> —*School Library Journal*

> "Even landlocked students can learn about the ocean and complete the activities in Oceans."
>
> —*Curriculum Review*

OCEANS

An Activity Guide for Ages 6–9

These more than 50 games, activities, and experiments are a boatful of fun whether you live in Cape Cod or in Kansas. Young children will delight in exploring different ocean habitats—from

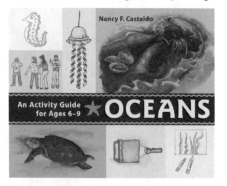

tide pools to sunlit waters to the deep-water world where light never penetrates—learning about sharks, sea turtles, dolphins, and much more.

$14.95 (CAN $22.95)
1-55652-443-9

Winter Day Play!

Activities, Crafts, and Games for Indoors and Out

Features more than 70 activities, crafts, and games that will keep kids busy learning, exploring, and having fun all winter long. Try Snow Painting with spray bottles filled with food coloring, building Snow Castles or a Japanese Snow Cottage, and Blowing Magic Bubbles and watching them freeze. If you don't get much snow or it's just too cold to go outside, find plenty of winter-inspired fun in making Eskimo Yo-Yos, holding a Marshmallow Sculpture Contest, or constructing a Snowflake Mobile.

$13.95 (CAN $20.95)
1-55652-381-5

A Smithsonian Notable Book

> "This one's a definite must for snow-bound families and teachers."
>
> —*Kids Home Library*

> "This terrific activity book is chock-full of wintertime projects for kids of all ages."
>
> —*Parents Guide*

CHICAGO REVIEW PRESS

Distributed by Independent Publishers Group

www.ipgbook.com

Available at your local bookstore or by calling 1-800-888-4741